Bernard Sesboüé

THE RESURRECTION AND THE LIFE

French text
translated by
Jane Burton

English text
edited by
Steven Heymans

A Liturgical Press Book

 THE LITURGICAL PRESS
Collegeville, Minnesota

Cover design by Greg Becker

This book was originally published in French by Desclée de Brouwer, Paris, France under the title *La Résurrection et la Vie: Petite catéchèse sur les choses de la fin* © 1990 by Desclée de Brouwer.

1   2   3   4   5   6   7   8

Library of Congress Cataloging-in-Publication Data

Sesboüé, Bernard, 1929–
    [Résurrection et la vie. English]
    The Resurrection and the life / Bernard Sesboüé ; French text translated by Jane Burton ; English text edited by Steven Heymans.
       p.   cm.
    Includes bibliographical references.
    ISBN 0-8146-2267-4
    1. Resurrection. 2. Future life—Christianity. 3. Catholic Church—Doctrines. I. Heymans, Steven. II. Title.
BT872.S4713   1996
236'.8—dc20   95-44528
                                                 CIP

Contents

Introduction

*"I believe
in the resurrection of the
body and life eternal."*
Apostles' Creed

The time is not so far away when authoritative voices judged that people of Western, "secular" society were no longer concerned with the ultimate questions of their existence. In our atheistic milieu, the temporal—the provisional horizon of the senses created by daily work, family, leisure activities, and commitment to the service of noble causes—was judged sufficient to constitute the happiness to which all human beings aspired, and to be the whole and sole measure of human value and moral grandeur. After all, do human beings really so need God and the promise of an eternal life in order to be, here and now, true persons in all their dignity?

Correlatively, Christian preaching about the "last things"[1] became more rare and gave way to an embarrassed silence. Several reasons may be cited for this trend. The once "great truths," which were concerned with the destiny of human beings after death, were too often preached in a way which evoked fear in order to bring

---

1. "Last things" is the classic term in Christian theology and preaching used to designate the realities which concern the final destiny of all humanity at the end of the world, and the ultimate fate of human beings after their death. The following form part of the preaching of the last things: the end of the world and the return of Christ, the resurrection, the universal judgment of humanity, and the particular judgment of each individual person. Today, in the wake of the biblical renewal movement, the Greek word "eschatology" is also used; this word is explained in chapter 1.

about "returns," that is to say, conversions. Descriptions of the sufferings of hell were given much emphasis. Ultimately, however, this approach had the long-term effect of a boomerang; not only did it not fail to scare, but it served to further augment the disaffection and derision of the faith. Adult human beings of an advanced society are no longer frightened by stories of bogeypersons.

Much of current theology is rightly concerned with Karl Marx's criticism of religion being the "opium of the people." By that, Marx means that religion often has a pacifying effect upon its adherents because of its emphasis upon the afterlife. In its effort to overcome this criticism, contemporary theology, and hence preaching, has emphasized a commitment to the temporal order through its promotion of social justice and human dignity. This orientation was founded on a theology of incarnation[2] which is perfectly legitimate in itself, but which was used exclusively, and which forgot the inevitable ruptures to which Christian salvation calls us.

Yet the horizon has changed with what is sometimes called "the fierce return of the religious." Paul Ricoeur, a preeminent philosopher of our time, had already diagnosed what he called the "retreat of the senses": "We will discover that what human beings lack most is justice, certainly; love, surely; but even more, significance. The insignificance of work, the insignificance of leisure, the insignificance of sexuality; these are the problems with which we are confronted."[3] At a time of rapid technological progress, human beings have less direction and purpose in life. Human beings, by nature, are not content with the temporal and provisional domains alone; we possess a transcendent dimension which is present in love relationships, in our major life choices and even in our work and leisure. Thus, even in these secular times, we find ourselves remarkably "religious." Yet, along with this hunger for the transcendent is a lack of religious and cultural roots. Too often, therefore, we turn to primitive and sometimes perverted religious expressions such as astrology, magic, esoterisms, or gnos-

---

2. Incarnational theology is a strain of Christian thought that affirms humanity through its emphasis on the incarnation (e.g., God becoming human). This affirmation means that Christians take earthly life and realities seriously as a way of preparing us for salvation.

3. Paul Ricoeur, *Esprit,* 346 (February 1966) 189.

THE RESURRECTION
AND THE LIFE

ticism,[4] as well as a host of sects vaguely inspired by Christianity and Eastern religions. Such sects range from those of genuine religious inspiration, to those which are exploitive of vulnerable people. It is in this context that the emergence of the belief in reincarnation, which has become a very popular answer to unanswerable questions, must be situated. Needless to say, this turning to sects as well as the popular belief in reincarnation poses a great challenge and problem for mainline Christian Churches.

This phenomenon urgently demands that we as Christians proclaim the mystery of eternal life promised to us in a way that can be understood and believed. We are leaving an era in which people were afraid to talk of death; we are increasingly preoccupied with the meaning of our own death, convinced that such understanding is necessary for a true understanding of the meaning of our lives. In reality, no one escapes during the course of life the ordeal of the death of those to whom they are close; to lose one's parents is always traumatic, even when they die at an old age. We are not only deeply wounded inwardly, but in the face of death, we are also put in the condition of becoming orphans. To lose a husband, a wife, a brother or sister, a dear friend, affects us even more harshly, as these are members of our own generation. Thus, to lose an infant is intolerable, for it is "contrary to nature." Children are the prolongation of ourselves into the future, and so to lose a child is all the more painful. The death of a loved one, whether from a grievous illness, an accident, or an inexplicable suicide, is always a scandal, and leads to a sense of aloneness, solitude, and sometimes a sense of culpability. It can be accompanied by a dark night of the soul, or it may occasion a loss of faith. Such spiritualism tempts us to find easy answers to complex problems through its flight-from-the-world, search-for-the-esoteric approach to life.

4. Astrology believes that the future depends on the conjunction of stars. Magic claims to affect, by rites and incantations, occult forces which govern the life of human beings. Esoterism is the desire for knowledge reserved solely for initiates, those who thus know essential secrets about life and the course of history. Gnosticism claims, by means of initiations and secret doctrines, to give access to supreme knowledge. Today all these different currents of thought have their own gurus and publications. One needs only to browse in the "New Age" section of most bookstores to see how popular the subject has become.

In these difficult times, many are scandalized by the words and attitudes of priests who are accused of uttering words which cause suffering and whose actions cause embarrassment. There also is, of course, the official teaching of the Church[5] which, in theory, serves as a corrective to the words and actions of priests when they are contrary to the gospel. Yet, to many, these teachings appear as abstract, irrelevant, self-contradicting, and a stranger to the scientific culture in which people are today immersed. Much of the language simply does not "get through." Its theological language is a block to the need people have to come to a sense of the "beyond."

Therefore, in these pages I should like to present as honestly as possible the principal elements of Christian faith in the resurrection of the body and eternal life. Faithful to the teachings of Scripture as presented in the tradition of the Church, and conscious of the extreme difficulty of the subject, I would also like to be attentive to the requests for a language capable of speaking to the needs of our contemporaries. My aim is to enlighten, but to do so without opening old wounds.

The subject of the last things has been treated by Scripture and the ancient tradition of the Church, above all, from a communitarian or collective point of view: those early Christians were concerned with the destiny of human history as viewed through the resurrection of Jesus, Christ and Lord; they were also concerned with proclaiming the resurrection of the body and the return of Christ, who would be the judge of the living and the dead. This theme will be the object of the first part of this book, for it will allow us to place these essential affirmations in a larger context. This proclamation also includes a concern for each person at the moment of death and the afterlife, for each of us has the stature of a person in the great body of humanity. From the time of the Middle Ages, the end-times have been examined from many perspectives: death, personal judgment, heaven, purgatory, and hell. All these will be the object of the second part of this book.

The writing of this book is solely my responsibility. Yet I wish to gratefully acknowledge the role of a several-year dialogue with

5. Teaching recalled by the Congregation for the Doctrine of the Faith in "Letter on Certain Questions Concerning Eschatology," *Documentation catholique,* no. 1769 (1979) 708–10.

the members of the Fraternity "Jonathan Pierres Vivantes" and those who accompany them from the shrine of Montiligeon. They have contributed greatly through their role in this dialogue. These men and women look beyond their own ordeal of having lost a child and help others face with loss through their charity, hope, and faith.

PART I

Resurrection
and
the End of the World

1

The End Already Present

Eschatology or Discourse about the End

Let us tame immediately the great technical word *eschatology*: it is discourse about that which is last or ultimate. When we use this word, therefore, we think automatically of what will happen at the end of history and at the return of Christ. This term orients us toward the future, and we may say with the theologian, Karl Rahner, that eschatology deals with the problem of the future. We are all geared and stretched toward the future. Put negatively, a "future without future" is a non-sense, a sort of death sentence. Youthfulness is seductive, for it represents the future, a future that one hopes will be infinitely better than the present. One dreams of the future in images of tomorrows; one prepares for it with all the strength of one's activity. The future is a point of flight which moves incessantly, like a mirage, but something we do not want to think of as simply unknowable. The future must lead to something other than a perpetual succession of time: we hope that it will open onto a stable present of a life which will never grow old. Our chasing of the future is at root the seeking of an end which will not be a simple limit, but the plenitude of a goal fully accomplished. A desire for something "definitive"— that is, eternal—is hidden in our attraction toward the future. Such an attraction can give sense and value to our lives and the loves which inspire it. In Christian language, this whole movement which carries human beings toward the future is called hope. Faith teaches us that the future is already inhabited by the gift of God.

The Event of Jesus Is an "Eschatological" Event

The mystery of Christian faith, the mystery of salvation for all human beings, founded in the event of the dead and risen Jesus, is profoundly eschatological. For not only is it oriented toward a future which God is preparing for human beings, but it also anticipates and realizes in part that future in the present. Jesus proclaimed the kingdom of God as both very near, present simply because he was present, and as future, as that which was promised by God. Jesus includes himself as part of God's promise at the end of time. Because the end time was thought to be near, there was some urgency about this message. But this was only a symbol of a greater urgency, that of the salvation of human beings, a salvation brought about by the direct intervention of God when he sent his Son to announce the Good News of forgiveness for all. What is urgently desired by God, as shown by this defining event, is our conversion.

In like manner, for the apostles, "if Jesus is risen, the end of the world is already here."[1] Paradoxically, what surprised the disciples, who were awaiting a general resurrection, was that Jesus alone was raised. For Jesus could only be raised as "the first fruits of those who have died" (1 Cor 15:20). The end of time had therefore become near in a qualitative manner, whatever the chronology to come, because "in these last days he has spoken to us by a Son" (Heb 1:2).

The Definitive Is Already Present

But is all this simply a game with words? Time continues and, from a historical point of view, who can predict the end? Yet of this we can be sure: Christian eschatological discourse does not aim to satisfy human curiosity by giving us a journalistic account of the end; it does this no more than scientific accounts of the origin of the world. What Christian faith tells us is that the "definitive," toward which we are journeying and which is the object of our hope, is already present as gift in our midst. To say that the end of history is anticipated in the resurrection of Jesus, which is a saving event, is to say that all human history

---

1. W. Pannenberg, *Esquisse d'une christologie* (Paris: Cerf, 1971) 73.

is saved. However, this is not to say that many are journeying toward a universal catastrophe or a universal perdition. In spite of sin and the risk that the free will of each person can take us on a path of destruction, humanity is on the way to succeeding; humanity and human history is progressing toward a blessed fulfillment in God. This success is inevitable; it was already given at the same time it was promised.

Thus, since the coming of Jesus, humanity lives in a tension between an already and a not yet. The transitory present of history and the gift which God destines for human beings beyond history are not realities that are exclusive of each other. Salvation is accomplished; the Spirit of God is given; the sacraments are given to allow human beings to live with eternal life. "Those who eat my flesh and drink my blood," says Jesus in St. John's Gospel, "have eternal life, and I will raise them up on the last day" (John 6:54). From now on, human beings can live by the grace of God, even if this remains largely hidden in our history and only manifests itself in discrete signs: "You have died, and your life is hidden with Christ in God. When Christ who is your life is revealed, then you also will be revealed with him in glory" (Col 3:3). Humanity must still pass through a "rupture" in order to enter into the fully manifested glory of God. At the same time, the life which is promised to us in God is none other than that which we already live: we *have* eternal life. There is no essential difference between the mystery of Christ lived today through grace, and the mystery of Christ in glory, where God will be manifested as all in all; the only difference is one of distance between that which is still in progress of being accomplished, but without any possibility of regression, and that which is totally accomplished.

Some time ago, after the second world war, Oscar Cullmann popularized this truth by using the eloquent image of J-day and V-day. J-day was that of the landing in Normandy and V-day was the day of final victory. From the moment the landing was successfully accomplished, one could consider that the war was won. Victory was inevitable. The war continued, however, with its cortege of dramas and deaths. It was only at V-day that the long-awaited peace could open onto an era of authentic happiness.

This insight must change our vision of both the present and the future life. The Christian is not caught in a false dualism of

---

Risen with Christ

So if you have been raised with Christ, seek the things that are above, where Christ is, seated at the right hand of God. Set your minds on things that are above, not on things that are on earth, for you have died, and your life is hidden with Christ in God. When Christ who is your life is revealed, then you also will be revealed with him in glory.

(Col 3:1-4)

---

two distinct realms in which we either commit ourselves to the temporal tasks, on the one hand, or to eternal life on the other. We are not limited to either a flat "horizontalism" on the one hand, or the service of an illusory "verticality" on the other. For if the definitive is already present, what we do here in the present must necessarily have a definitive value, and may enter into the great movement of salvation. No longer is there a rupture between time and eternity: through Christ, time has given birth to an eternal salvation. Are our individual human liberties also capable of committing themselves to an eternal project?

How to Speak of Definitive Realities

If we wish to speak of eschatology, we must translate the mystery which we are already living, and which would have no meaning if we had "for this life only we have hoped in Christ" (1 Cor 15:19), into the terms of eternity. Yet here we face a formidable problem of language. Our language is based on the multitude of experiences that we have in our earthly time and space. It is always supported by images and representations which help us think. Yet religious language tries to express the connection between human beings and God's world; in order to do this it must translate words and experiences of this world into a transcendent realm. Religious events always happen in the context of human history, not in a purely external realm. Far from negating, history affirms religious experience and events. At the same time, religious understandings of events cannot be limited by human history, which generally does not lend itself to religious interpretations of events.

Ideas and words taken from earthly time and space fail utterly when they are used to express the two passages from eternity to time and from time to eternity which are the creation and the end of the world. And yet we can neither think nor speak without using human words and images. Christian faith and revelation must also use human words and representations insofar as they are human discourse. But the representations thus become *symbols,* the word being understood here in a full and strong sense. These symbols are present in accounts which one may call mythical, not in order to underrate them, but in order to underscore that their meaning is found beyond the materiality of the history which they recount. It is thus that the eschatological representations of the Bible seek to express the last, "definitive" encounter of humanity with God. This final encounter is expressed in the words used for all the encounters which we have experienced in our earthly world and history.

The Great Biblical Images

Certain biblical images belong to the literary genre of apocalyptic, that is, are the result of a vision experienced by a prophet or a writer. Such biblical references describe, in various accounts, what will happen in the end times which will usher in the definitive triumph of Christ. These accounts announce trials and calamities, which are the signs of the exacerbation of the drama between two opposing forces, in which we have the sinful freedom of human beings on the one hand, and God's desire for human and cosmic salvation on the other. It is thus that Jesus, in the Synoptic Gospels (Matt 24:1-44; Mark 13:1-35; Luke 17:17, 23-35; 21:5-31), calls us to be vigilant in announcing the great tribulations that will precede the event of the Son of Man. It is thus that the Revelation of John describes the eschatological trials of the Church that will take place before the wedding of the Lamb. Yet, the apocalyptic description goes beyond the images of cosmic cataclysm by pointing to a glorious and peaceful manifestation of the Son of Man. Revelation mentions the judgment, announces the definitive victory of the Messiah, and culminates in the blessed vision of the new heaven and earth. By using familiar biblical terms and images (Rev 21), Revelation describes the new Jerusalem, a city in which God dwells with human beings in total harmony. Similarly, at the sound of God's trumpet, Paul describes the resurrection of the dead as an immense reckoning of gathered humanity before Christ (1 Thess 4:13-17). Heavenly life is described here either in the image of a glorious liturgy celebrated around God's throne (Rev 7:9-17), or as a festive meal, analogous to our wedding banquets. There are other positive images which would have spoken powerfully to the people of the time: rest, in contrast to the daily toil for simple survival; coolness, in a place of desert heat and dryness; light, in a time without electricity; feasting and celebration, in a time of daily struggle. All these images are significant, for they eternalize those rare moments of intense human happiness and love.

In these first eschatological reflections, a key word, *resurrection,* is often repeated. A word linked to that of *life,* Christian eschatology promises us life through resurrection. The word *resurrection* brings us to a critical moment in which we must ask: How does biblical thought explain this intense hope in the resurrection? What meaning must we give to the resurrection of Christ? How must we understand our own resurrection?

Apocalyptic Vision of the End

Then I saw a new heaven and a new earth, for the first heaven and the first earth had passed away, and the sea was no more. And I saw the holy city, the new Jerusalem, coming down out of heaven from God, prepared as a bride adorned for her husband. And I heard a loud voice from the throne saying,

> *"See, the home of God is among mortals.*
> *He will dwell with them as their God;*
> *they will be his peoples,*
> *and God himself will be with them;*
> *he will wipe every tear from their eyes.*
> *Death will be no more;*
> *mourning and crying and pain will be no more,*
> *for the first things have passed away."*

(Rev 21:1-5)

2

The Genesis of Faith in the Resurrection

It was later rather than sooner that the Old Testament announced the resurrection of human beings. Over time, a hermeneutic developed whose object of discourse was that of resurrection and afterlife; this development went hand in hand with other interpretive developments. This progression can be schematized in three great stages.

Primitive Belief: "Sheol" or the Depths of Oblivion

Life is the greatest gift to human beings, and death appears as the catastrophe *par excellence*. However, all is not ended with death. At death human beings go to "sheol"—the underworld or the depths, the Jewish equivalent of the Greek "hades," a place of darkness (Job 10:21-22), of dust (Job 17:16), of silence (Ps 94:17), a prison furnished with gates (Jonah 2:7; Job 38:17), where the shades lead an insubstantial life like a dismal sleep (Dan 12:2), sharing a miserable condition close to inexistence (Job 7:8-21). Sheol is not a place of punishment, but a place of perdition, "the place of oblivion." It is a place where human beings can no longer know God; where love, wisdom, and life are no more:

> Do you work wonders for the dead?
>   Do the shades rise up to praise you?
> Is your steadfast love declared in the grave,
>   or your faithfulness in Abad'don?

> Are your wonders known in the darkness,
>   or your saving help in the land of forgetfulness?

(Ps 88:10-13).

From this land no one returns; no one rises up again (Job 10:21); such is the inexorable law.

This conception of sheol is the transposition of images traditionally linked with the sepulchre—the place of the tomb where corpses return to the womb of the earth. Sheol is a mythical place, one which had a firm grasp on the imaginations of people at that time. Just as the body, which appears to sleep, disintegrates, so the breath of life wears itself out in a sleep deprived of all happiness. The dead are destined to oblivion, as no one has come back from the grave. The notion of sheol is an accumulation of dramatic experiences of death from time immemorial.

In such a perspective, human hope remains tied to earthly life. For example, God's great promise is the calm and prosperous possession of a fertile land (Deut 7:12-15; 8:7-10). Likewise, what is considered a great catastrophe is to die prematurely, "not having had one's fill of days." Since human beings must go to sheol, their sole way of surviving is to have numerous children, to prolong themselves through the lives of those who have been born from their substance. Such is the first victory over death: "When your days are fulfilled and you lie down with your ancestors, I will raise up your offspring after you, who shall come forth from your body, and I will establish his kingdom" (2 Sam 7:12).

But Where Is Justice?

This primitive notion of the rewards of a long life eventually raises the question of justice. One would expect God's blessings of a long and fruitful life to be bestowed upon those who honored the covenant, and that a premature death was a form of punishment upon the wicked. Yet experience shows that death strikes blindly, without distinction: the just are afflicted, persecuted or die, while hoards of the wicked prosper with impunity.

What does one gain by invoking God?

Why do the wicked live on,
reach old age, and grow mighty in power?
Their children are established in their presence,
and their offspring before their eyes.
Their houses are safe from fear,
and no rod of God is upon them.
Their bull breeds without fail;
their cow calves and never miscarries.
They send out their little ones like a flock,
and their children dance around.
They sing to the tambourine and the lyre,
and rejoice to the sound of the pipe.
They spend their days in prosperity,
and in peace they go down to Sheol.
They say to God, "Leave us alone!
We do not desire to know your ways.
What is the Almighty, that we should serve him?
And what profit do we get if we pray to him?"
Is not their prosperity indeed their own achievement?
The plans of the wicked are repugnant to me.
(Job 21:7-16)

Such is the formidable problem of justice posed by the book of Job, written about 400 B.C.[1] In the midst of his trial of immense unhappiness, Job protests his innocence and his righteousness; he rejects the easy words of his well-meaning questioners who try to persuade him to recognize his own culpability. His suffering leads him to the brink of revolt: "Why do the wicked live on,/ reach old age, and grow mighty in power?/ Their children are established in their presence,/ and their offspring before their eyes" (Job 21:7-8). Why is it, Job asks, that "the wicked are spared in the day of calamity?" (30)? Why, for that matter, serve God at all: "What is the Almighty, that we should serve him?/and what profit do we get if we pray to him? . . . You say, 'God

---

1. God's justice is only thought of here from the angle of the question of retribution. The idea of God's merciful, "justifying justice" will be looked at later, pp. 82–91.

stores up their iniquity for their children' " (15-19). Although Job's questions are echoed and somewhat answered in the Psalms, the answers are not satisfying. There is much mystery to Job's simple, but honest question.

Sin and the trials of death had always been the explanation for why some end up in the depths of the underworld. The underground dwelling was always explained as a place of suffering, a place for those who participated in a revolt against creation. To describe the underworld, an image of fire is often invoked; this image recalls the perpetual fire which burns the refuse in the valley of Gehenna, the place at the foot of Jerusalem. Worms, which gnaw at the putrid flesh of sinners, are another image used to describe the underworld. Of course people of the time took much consolation in knowing this was a place reserved for the wicked, and not the just. God's justice rested upon this.

The Presentiments of the Prophets

With time, a series of breaches began to break open the traditional conception of sheol. The Canticle of Anne already affirms the almighty power of God over life and death: "The Lord kills and brings to life; he brings down to Shē'ōl and raises up" (1 Sam 2:6). Elijah and Elishah perform resurrections (1 Kgs 17:17, 24; 2 Kgs 4:31-37; 13:21). These references express God's strength over death, since he is capable of giving back life. Amos asserts that God has power over sheol itself (Amos 9:2; cf. Ps 139:8). "O Death, where are your plagues?/ O Shē'ōl, where is your destruction?" says Hosea (13:14). When King Hezekiah is on the verge of death, God, through the mouth of Isaiah, tells Hezekiah that, because of his prayer, fifteen years will be added to his life (Isa 38:5). Here, God's answer to Hezekiah seems consistent with the theology of sheol. Yet, in the canticle, Hezekiah expresses thanksgiving for his deliverance from death: "Surely it was for my welfare/ that I had great bitterness;/ but you have held back my life from the pit of destruction,/ for you have cast all my sins behind your back (Isa 38:17). There is another development in Ezekiel 37 for whom "resurrection" means the restoration of the people of Israel to the land promised in the covenant, as opposed to the resurrection of the dead. There is a similar thought in Isaiah in which he says, "The dead do not live;/ shades do not rise—because you have punished and destroyed them,/ and wiped out all memory of them. . ." (Isa 26:14). It is here that a development in the understanding of sheol begins—from that of a neutral preserve of the dead, to a place of punishment for the wicked.

Even Isaiah's lot, though harsh and pitiable, is but a veiled promise of resurrection.[2] For even though "They made his grave with the wicked . . . he shall see his offspring, and shall prolong his days;/ through him the will of the Lord shall prosper" (Isa 53:9-11). Thus Yahweh is a God for whom our servanthood can take many forms.

The Formal Witness of the Last Writings of the Old Testament

It is only in the most recent books of the Old Testament that a clear affirmation of the resurrection is found. In these witnesses, the Jewish apocalyptic[3] tradition holds an important place.

In this late literary genre, the book of Daniel affirms both a general resurrection, as well as a retribution which takes two forms: one to life and another to shame. Thus the notion of sheol undergoes a transformation from that of an underworld preserve, to that of hell as we currently understand it:

> In those days your people will be saved, whoever's name is written in the Book. And the crowd of those who sleep in the dust will awake, some to eternal life, others to shame and eternal reprobation. The wise will shine like the splendor of the firmament; and those who have led many to righteousness will shine like stars—forever and eternally.
>
> (Dan 12:1-3)

2. The Servant of God is the mysterious figure announced in four texts of the second part of the book of Isaiah which dates from the exile. After the failure of the kings and priests, salvation was seen as something realized by this completely faithful person, who would be despised, rejected, and put to death. Christians will see in this figure the announcement of Jesus, delivered up in his passion.

3. The word *apocalypse* signifies revelation. *Apocalypse* is the name given to a literary genre that developed after the exile. The writers of apocalyptic literature proclaimed the final victory of God and of the elect by means of

The persecution of Israel by Antiochus Epiphanes in the second century B.C. greatly contributed to this development. It posed acutely the problem of retribution. What would be the lot of Israel's martyrs? The answer is perfectly clear: God, the creator, capable of forming life in the womb of a woman, is also God the re-creator, capable of giving life definitively. The mother of seven brothers who were successively martyred expresses this thought before her sons: "Therefore the Creator of the world, who shaped the beginning of humankind and devised the origin of all things, will in his mercy give life and breath back to you again, since you now forget yourselves for the sake of his laws" (2 Macc 7:23).

The wisdom tradition is also in line with such a vision. Yet the book of Wisdom, the text most markedly influenced by Greek culture, prefers to use the language of the immortality of the soul. However, "soul" must be understood not only as a metaphysical principle, but also as the breath of life and a principle of personality:

> But the souls of the righteous are in the hand of God,
> and no torment will ever touch them.
> In the eyes of the foolish they seemed to have died,
> and their departure was thought to be a disaster,
> and their going from us to be their destruction;
> but they are at peace.
> For though in the sight of others they were punished,
> their hope is full of immortality.
> Having been disciplined a little, they will receive great good,
> because God tested them and found them worthy of himself;
> like gold in the furnace he tried them,
> and like a sacrificial burnt offering he accepted them. . . .
> (Wis 3:1-7)
> But the righteous, though they die early, will be at rest.
> For old age is not honored for length of time . . .
> There were some who pleased God and were loved by him. . . .
> Being perfected in a short time, they fulfilled long years;
> for their souls were pleasing to the Lord,
> therefore he took them quickly from the midst of wickedness.
> (Wis 4:7-14)

---

revelations, fantastic visions, and scenarios of mighty combats between God's messengers and the forces of evil. They were writings of encouragement and hope for believers in the midst of persecutions.

One notices in this text a fundamental shift in emphasis from ancient ideas about the value and blessing of a long life, to that of a life lived in righteousness. A premature death is no longer a misfortune; rather it is the mark of love for God and liberation from a world inhabited by evil. Thus in the Old Testament we find a clear affirmation of "eternal life."

The doctrine of the resurrection of the dead spread rapidly and widely in Israel in the first century before Christ. At the threshold of the New Testament, it became the common possession of Judaism, even if the Sadducean sect rejected it, as shown by their posing the question to Jesus of the woman who had seven husbands (Matt 22:23-28). In any case, it was the groundwork laid by Judaism of the expectation of a general resurrection (cf. John 11:24) which paved the way for an eventual understanding of the resurrection of Jesus.

An Itinerary of Mystical Discovery

Protect me, O God, for in you I take refuge.
I say to the Lord, "You are my Lord;
I have no good apart from you."

The LORD *is my chosen portion and my cup;*
you hold my lot.
The boundary lines have fallen for me in pleasant places;
I have a goodly heritage.

I bless the LORD *who gives me counsel;*
in the night also my heart instructs me.
I keep the LORD *always before me;*
because he is at my right hand, I shall not be moved.

Therefore my heart is glad, and my soul rejoices;
my body also rests secure.
For you do not give me up to Shẽ'ōl,
or let your faithful one see the Pit.

You show me the path of life.
In your presence there is fullness of joy;
in your right hand are pleasures forevermore.

(Ps 16:1, 2, 5-11)

The Fruit of a Triple Thrust[4]

This evolving theology of revelation leads to the idea of the resurrection and immortality of human beings primarily in three ways.

The first way is *love*: the spiritual life of the Jewish people is one which desires to live intimately with God, without interruption and without end (cf. Ps 16; 49:73). Human beings have been created in the image and likeness of God, and their most profound desire is to live always in communion with him.

The second thrust, as we have seen, is that of *justice*: the theology of sheol presupposed an equality between persons, whatever their actions had been. This, of course, was in tension with notions of divine justice and contradicted the hope of the martyrs as well.

The third thrust was that of *life*: the God of creation is also a God who recreates. This God of life is stronger than death. This historical sketch of the development of our understanding of resurrection in the Old Testament is not unlike the kind of personal faith challenges through which each of us must pass. We, too, must come to terms with the reality of death, for the fact that it will eventually make orphans of each one of us evokes strong feelings of abandonment; we, too, must not be paralyzed in the face of our own death by recognizing the life beyond this life, and by embodying the hope that comes with this recognition.

4. I am indebted to the exegete P.-E. Bonnard for these ideas.

3

The Home of Light:
The Resurrection of Christ

Jesus Heals the Sick and Raises the Dead

Jesus begins his public ministry by doing several things: through his ministry of healing, forgiveness, and reconciliation, he proclaims the coming of God's kingdom; he proclaims the beatitudes, the charter of this kingdom; and he tells stories, usually in the form of parables, so that his followers might better understand the Good News and be converted.

Yet the kingdom which he announces in words he also inaugurates by acts, the most important of which are, without doubt, his willingness to eat at the table of sinners, and his eagerness to forgive sins (Matt 9:2; Luke 7:48). Such acts, of course, scandalized some. Jesus' forgiveness of sins seemed often tied to the health of the body. He is not insensitive to human suffering—whether it be health or that which deprives us of liberty. His healing miracles are also signs of the kingdom; their purpose is to liberate human beings, to reveal what we should be, and to give us the fullness of life and happiness—in a word, to save us. If sickness is a mysterious sign of the disorder and sin which dwell within us, the healing of bodies is also a sign of the liberation from sin, a gift of human freedom (Mark 2:10-11).

This clear link between bodily healing and forgiveness of sins, however, must not take away from the practical importance of healing. To appreciate the importance of physical healing, one may consider the three resurrection accounts reported in the Gospels—that of the son of the widow of Nain (Luke 7:11-17), that of the daughter of Jairus (Luke 8:49-56), and that of Lazarus (John 11:1-44) as extreme forms of healing. Sickness is a pre-eminent sign of death, which it sometimes leads to. When Jesus does not arrive in time to stop it in its tracks, he, as it were, makes it retrace its steps; that is, he gives back life to those who have crossed the frontier of death.

In healing and raising people from the dead, Jesus gives a simple and eloquent answer to the question: in what does the kingdom of God consist? Those who believe regain health and life. Their bodies are saved. Such healings are "messianic" proclamations of what the Messiah-Savior is capable of doing. They have a symbolic value and announce in their own way what the saved world will be like, a world constituted by victory of life over death. Through them, we see that the salvation brought by Jesus affects our whole being, including our physical well-being. The three resurrections mentioned above tell us that the salvation Jesus offers includes resurrection.

This attention of Jesus to bodies invites us to be attentive to the role of his own body. All that Jesus says and does passes by his body: his word passes by his human voice; the healings pass by the touch of his hand. Thus the health he brings passes from his own body to sick, and even dead, bodies. What will be the role, therefore, of Jesus' own body, once he has passed, like every human being, through the law of death?

Jesus Has Changed the Meaning of Death

Jesus cannot rise without passing through the trial of death. If he had not done so, he would not have really shared our human condition, and thus his resurrection, insofar as this word could still have a meaning in such a hypothesis, would have no relevance for us. He, the innocent one, the human being without sin, assumed the condition of sinful humanity; he accepted the agony and scandal of death in all its obscurity. The link between death and sin was evident to him, for his death was the result of the sinful violence of human beings. Jesus experienced in his flesh the truth that sin leads to death.

By loving to the end those who were his own in the world, Jesus changed the meaning of death. Just as all his existence had been an "existence for" his Father and his human sisters and brothers, so too his death was a "death for us," in loving, filial

I am the Resurrection and the Life

Martha said to Jesus:
"Lord, if you had been here, my brother would not have died.
But even now I know that God will give whatever you ask of him."
Jesus said to her,
"Your brother will rise again."
Martha said to him, "I know that he will rise again in the resur-
rection on the last day."
Jesus said to her,
"I am the resurrection and the life. Those who believe in me, even
though they die, will live, and everyone who lives and believes in
me will never die."

(John 11:21-26)

obedience to the Father, who himself was giving his Son. His death was a battle—a battle of love with hate, of the uniting powers of forgiveness with the dividing power of lies and violence, of life with death. Death was conquered in the very moment of its apparent triumph; the death of Jesus is a work of life which he gives to us. Jesus placed his life in the hands of the Father so that the Father might give it back to him as the fruit of salvation for all human beings. Such is the true sense of what is called the sacrifice of Christ.

Jesus Is Truly Risen

With the resurrection of Jesus we arrive at the heart of the Christian message about human beings and their salvation. "If Christ has not been raised," writes St. Paul, "your faith is futile and you are still in your sins" (1 Cor 15:17). It is not the object of this book to lay out in detail the theological meaning of the resurrection of Jesus, the nature of faith, its relationship with history, nor its christological significance.[1] My aim is only to underline the "eschatological" significance of the resurrection.

To begin with, it must be pointed out that, in rising, Jesus has not returned to his former state of life. The mode by which

1. Cf. on this point, B. Sesboüé, *Jesus-Christ dans la tradition de l'Église* (Paris: Desclée, 1982).

he manifested himself to his disciples has changed; it is no longer one of continuous companionship, but sudden and gratuitous encounters which escape the laws of our space and time. Of course, the risen Jesus let himself be seen by his disciples in a form adapted to the fact that they were not yet risen. But the evident discontinuity, in spite of a real continuity, between the state of the pre-paschal Jesus and his risen condition, tells us that Jesus has passed beyond the limits of our history, that he is no longer susceptible to death (Rom 6:9), and that his humanity has attained in God definitive life.

A second point is equally essential: the resurrection concerns the totality of the person of Jesus before Easter, including his mortal body.[2] This is the reason why Jesus wishes to make himself known by the bodily senses of the disciples: "he was seen" (1 Cor 15:5-8), touched, and ate and drank with them (cf. Luke 24:39-43). He is not a pure spirit or a ghost.

But it was also important that the bodily resurrection of Jesus was empirically demonstrated through the disappearance of his body. This is the significance of finding the tomb open and empty. It is not essentially a proof of the resurrection, but an important sign both in fact and in sense for, in Jewish anthropology, the body is the person. It can be said that the proclamation of the resurrection "could not have stood up for a day, nor even an hour, in Jerusalem, if the emptiness of the tomb had not been a well-attested fact to all those concerned."[3] In his preaching at Pentecost, Peter made appeal to the fact that "He was not abandoned to Hades/ nor did his flesh experience corruption" (Acts 2:31, citing Ps 16:10). The empty tomb is a pregnant sign announcing nothing less than the eschatological transformation of the world. It says to us that the present state of the world is not its definitive reality, that corruption will not have the last word about the human condition, for the cosmos in the person of Jesus has already known a rupture, the completion of which must make the universe transparent to God's life.

2. On the paradoxical nature of the risen or spiritual body, cf. the analysis of the text of 1 Corinthians 15 in the chapter on the resurrection of the flesh.

3. W. Pannenberg, citing P. Althaus, *Esquisse d'une christologie* (Paris: Cerf, 1971) 117.

These points are decisive *for us,* as Christians, for the resurrection of Jesus portends our own resurrection. As he was raised, so we shall be raised. This message of resurrection for us is profoundly eschatological, for it represents the "definitive," that is, what our definitive future state will be.

The Definitive Victory of Life Over Death

The resurrection of Jesus constitutes, then, a definitive victory over death, considered both as the destiny of human beings and as the consequence of their sin. Death is the enemy *par excellence* of human beings; it is allied with the powers of evil, sin, and hell. This inexorable reign of death over humanity has a very firm grasp, yet it no longer has the last word. From now on, God is the one who has raised Jesus from the dead, and therefore the one who is capable of raising all the dead. The resurrection of Jesus reveals to us God's plan for every human being.

This victory over death also tells us that Christian salvation consists in life, for God is the God of the living and not the God of the dead, as Jesus strongly affirms in the face of the Sadducees (Matt 22:32). It is concerned with the life of human beings, with the human condition in which we live out our existence. But it also concerns the life of God which is communicated to us definitively, without suppressing that which is human. For our "divinization" is also the summit of our "humanization;" the divine fulfills the human by giving it knowledge, freedom, love, and therefore happiness. The divine brings to us an added dimension of personal relations between all the members of the great family of God. This, now, is an eternal life which will no longer be subject to aging, sickness, and death.

We can therefore understand the insistence of John's Gospel in telling us that in the Word was life (John 1:4), that "whoever believes in the Son has eternal life" (3:36), that the Son of Man gives "the food that endures for eternal life" (6:27), and that his flesh is the bread given so that the world may have life (6:51). Peter can thus confess before him: "Lord, to whom can we go? You have the words of eternal life" (6:68). Lastly, Jesus indentifies himself with life: "I am the resurrection and the life" (11:25).

He Is Risen for Us

Just as Jesus died "for our trespasses," he is raised "for our justification" (Rom 4:25). There would have been no reason to become incarnate if it had not been "for us"; no reason to die except "for us," no reason to be raised except "for us."

This "for us" is already fully actual: through baptism we have already entered into the death and resurrection of Christ (cf. Rom 6:1-11). Paul's language changes here, however, as if he does not succeed in synthesizing in a single formula all the aspects of this mysterious reality. At one moment he speaks of our death with Christ as a past event, and of our resurrection as a future event: "For if we have been united with him in a death like his, we will certainly be united with him in a resurrection like his" (Rom 6:5). At other times he speaks of this resurrection in the past: "You have been raised with Christ" (Col 3:1; 2:12), and even of our ascension to heaven as a passed event: "But God . . . who made us . . . and raised us up with him and seated us with him in the heavenly places in Christ Jesus. . . ." Thus by grace, the resurrection of Jesus already has its full effect in us, but "your life is hidden with Christ in God" (Col 3:3). It must pass through other stages until its full manifestation.

For this "for us" still has a future: the resurrection of Jesus must end in our definitive resurrection. This resurrection will occur in two stages: from the moment of our death we shall live with the Lord (2 Cor 5:8). That is why Paul dares to say: "For me, living is Christ and dying is gain" (Phil 1:21). His whole life is stretched toward the future, to the appropriation of the mystery of Christ: "I want to know Christ and the power of his resurrection and the sharing of his sufferings by becoming like him in his death, if somehow I may attain the resurrection from the dead" (Phil 3:10-11). The second stage of this resurrection will accompany the victory of all those who have died in Christ.[4]

He Descended into Hell

Included in the Apostles' Creed is a reference to Jesus' descent into hell. Although this assertion sounds odd at face value,

---

4. See chapters 7–8.

it makes sense when hell is understood in light of the mythical image of sheol: "For Christ also suffered for sins once for all, the righteous for the unrighteous, in order to bring you to God. He was put to death in the flesh, but made alive in the spirit, in which also he went and made a proclamation to the spirits in prison, who in former times did not obey, when God waited patiently . . ." (1 Pet 3:18-20).

The early Church fathers took up this theme, which allowed them to reply to the agonizing question: how could Christ save the multitude of human beings who had preceded him on earth? (This question corresponds to that which we spontaneously ask today: how is Christ able to save the human beings who come into the world so long after him?) Jesus descends into hell to liberate those who are there; he proclaims the good news of their salvation; he goes to affirm his victory over death in the very place of the dead, which is the beginning of resurrection for them. Ignatius of Antioch writes thus: "The prophets, being his disciples in spirit, waited for him as their master. . . . By his presence he had raised them from death."[5] Irenaeus takes up the same idea: "And this is why the Lord descended into the lower depths of the earth, so as to bring the good news of his coming to those there, he who is the remission of sins for those who believe in him."[6]

Thus, under this image which for us is strange, but which we can understand better in the light of the biblical tradition, the universality of salvation is announced to us, through Christ's act of redemption for those in hell. Jesus had put an end to the reality of sheol. Salvation is offered to all those who desire it. Thus our understanding of hell is no longer one of "the depths," but one of a place for those who choose to radically reject Christ and his Spirit.

Our Hope of Resurrection

Can people today still believe in the resurrection? To answer this it helps to note that Jesus' immediate disciples most likely

5. Ignatius of Antioch, *Letters* (Paris: Cerf, 1969) 10:105.
6. Irenaeus of Lyons, *Against the Heresies,* trans. D. J. Unger (New York: Paulist, 1992).

believed in a general resurrection of the dead, as articulated in the Jewish apocalyptic tradition. However, for modern persons, this is no longer the case; we're more likely to regard such a doctrine as a quaint, but unscientific notion from an ancient mythological past. Thus, is it even possible to make the doctrine of the resurrection credible to people of our time?

In trying to respond to this serious question, we must avoid wholesale dismissals of the spiritual impoverishment of modern, secular society. For, as Wolfhart Pannenberg has said, "Without doubt, one can consider as an anthropological reality, of universal value, the assertion that the natural destiny of human beings does not find its definitive fulfilment in the finitude of their terrestrial life."[7] The philosophical reflection of the Marxist-humanist, Ernest Bloch, follows the same idea: "The derisory acknowledgment of nothingness does not easily suffice to keep the head high and to act as if there would be no end. On the contrary, there are clear indications which show that images of more ancient and more comforting desires exist in the subconscious and provide a sustaining support."[8]

Thus human beings appear to be inhabited by an incorrigible hope; indeed, as Karl Rahner has said, human beings are those who have "the boldness" to hope: "It belongs to the nature of a conscious human being to hope beyond death."[9] In the language which is proper to him, Karl Rahner speaks of a "transcendental" hope of resurrection, a hope which inhabits the constant interior movement within each person toward the greatest and the best. Vis-à-vis this hope, which is not necessarily conscious, each of us reacts by an acceptance or a refusal of a definitive meaning to life which is also life. The one who has an accepting attitude will thus be open to the proclamation of the resurrection, provided that this proclamation is given within the context of a faith which itself gives signs of the truth of such a proclamation.

7. W. Pannenberg, *Equisse d'une christologie* (Paris: Cerf, 1971) 95.
8. Ibid., 96.
9. W. Pannenberg, ibid., 97.

4

The Resurrection
of the Body

The salvation brought by Jesus Christ proclaims the resurrection of the body, itself prefigured by the resurrection of Jesus. The "resurrection of the dead" or the "resurrection of the body" are formally expressed in the third article of the Creed at which we must now look through the light of Paul's letter to the Corinthians (1 Cor 15). We must also define what a resurrected body could be, as well as how it might be represented. We must also compare and contrast the Christian understanding of resurrection with that of reincarnation, as understood by many spiritualists today.

St. Paul and the Resurrection of the Dead (1 Cor 15)

The resurrection of the dead was a concept particularly difficult to accept for Greeks for whom the law of death was unchangeable and universal.

Besides, the body belongs to the realm of the transitory, subject to degeneration and corruption; it is a place of human fragility and misery. In contrast, human grandeur resides in the spiritual dimension: the immortality of the soul is the greatest thing for which mortals may hope. We are aware of the mixed reactions to Paul at the Areopagus of Athens, where, at the end of a speech well-adapted to the religious sense of the Athenians, he made a brief mention of the resurrection of Jesus: "At the word 'resurrection from the dead' some mocked, others declared: 'We will hear you again about this' " (Acts 17:32). The same difficulty was found in the Greek community of Corinth in which some of its members argued against the resurrection from the dead.

In this situation Paul reacts with the strongest possible force. He reminds those who criticize his confession of faith "that he was raised on the third day in accordance with the scriptures" (1 Cor 15:4). He emphasizes the contradiction between Christian faith in the resurrection of Christ and the notion that there is no resurrection of the dead. He even explores the logic of there being no resurrection which, he concludes, would render Christianity devoid of content and validity. Moreover, if such were the case, the apostolic witness would be a lie, the salvation brought by Christ would be an illusion, and Christians would be forever imprisoned in their sin.

Thus Paul vigorously reaffirms the resurrection of Jesus which he links to the resurrection of the dead: "But in fact Christ has been raised from the dead, the first fruits of those who have died" (1 Cor 15:20). Just as Adam, the first man, was cause of death for all humanity because of his sin, so Christ, the new man, is cause of life for all because of his resurrection. And Paul evokes the end of time when the Son, surrounded by the risen and the just, will give back sovereignty to his Father, once death, the last enemy, has been conquered.

However, the mere repeating of the apostolic faith is not sufficient. One must satisfy the curiosity of the Corinthians: "But someone will ask, 'How are the dead raised? With what kind of body do they come?' " (1 Cor 15:35). This question posed by the Corinthians is also the question posed by us today: how is such a thing possible? How must it be understood?

Paul replies in making a comparison: there is a total disproportion between the tiny seed and the opulence of the plant, or tree, about which Paul is talking. The transition from one to the other is an astonishing process of the grain which dies and dissolves in the soil; it is reduced to nothing before giving place to the totally new body of the plant. As Paul and his contemporaries are ignorant of the biological process from one to the other, the movement of the process is the immediate expression of the almighty power of God which makes amazing bodies spring forth from the rottenness of the seed. It is clearly a miracle. Paul also admires the differentiation of species, rigorously respected over the cycle of generations. From the plant seed, Paul uses the example of an animal seed, which, by an analogous process in the female body, is compared to the womb of the earth which constructs a new living body according to each species of human beings, beasts, birds, and fish.

Paul then applies his comparison to the resurrection of the dead: "What is sown is perishable, what is raised is imperishable. It is sown in dishonor, it is raised in glory. It is sown in weakness, it is raised in power. It is sown a physical body, it is raised a spiritual body" (1 Cor 15:42-44).

Paul compares our bodily existence to that of a seed for, once dead, both are in the earth. Resurrection, like the germination and growth of plants from seeds, is a miraculous event. Eventually, however, Paul introduces a break with this comparison: there comes a time when we leave our "animal being," which we are today, to take on the spiritual being that we will be in the risen Christ. As Paul says, while the "animal body" is perishable, the "spiritual body" is glorious, heavenly, and imperishable: "For this perishable body puts on imperishability, and this mortal body puts on immortality."

Is such an argument still valid for us today? For we know the complex biological processes of animals and plants. And we know the conditions from which animal and vegetable bodies are generated. These realities are no longer miracles for us. It would be a mistake to try to imagine an analogous biological process, still undiscovered, through which the resurrection of the dead could be explained.

However, whatever the scientific explanation proper to each process, our faith can recognize in this marvellous movement of life the creative action of God who brings it to birth. Life is in itself a "miracle"—an eminently improbable miracle according to the order of probability—just as the whole of creation is a miracle. We are also better informed, through scientific knowledge itself, of the radical difference between the intercosmic processes and the fact of the resurrection, which by definition transcends our universe. What we know allows us to believe in the unknown, and in a certain measure, to think of it. With the acorn and the oak tree, biology gives us the means by which to know how one develops into the other. In the case of the resurrection, however, there is no discipline to explain for us how God brings the dead to life. But we do know that the one who has the power to create, also has the power to recreate.

A Spiritual Body

But someone will ask, "How are the dead raised? What kind of body will they become?" Fool! What you sow does not come to life unless it dies. And as for what you sow, you do not sow the body that is to be, but a bare seed, perhaps of wheat or of some other grain. But God gives it a body as he has chosen, and to each kind of seed its own body. Not all flesh is alike, but there is one flesh for human beings, another for animals, another for birds, and another for fish. There are both heavenly bodies and earthly bodies, but the glory of the heavenly is one thing, and that of the earthly is another. There is one glory of the sun, and another glory of the moon, and another glory of the stars; indeed, star differs from star in glory.

So it is with the resurrection of the dead. What is sown is perishable, what is raised is imperishable. It is sown in dishonor, it is raised in glory. It is sown in weakness, it is raised in power. It is sown a physical body, it is raised a spiritual body. If there is a physical body, there is also a spiritual body. Thus it is written, "The first man, Adam, became a living being"; the last Adam became a life-giving spirit. But it is not the spiritual that is first, but the physical, and then the spiritual. The first man was from the earth, a man of dust; the second man is from heaven. As was the man of dust, so are those who are of the dust; and as is the man of heaven, so are those who are of heaven. Just as we have borne the image of the man of dust, we will also bear the image of the man of heaven.

What I am saying, brothers and sisters, is this: flesh and blood cannot inherit the kingdom of God, nor does the perishable inherit the imperishable. Listen, I will tell you a mystery! We will not all die, but we will all be changed, in a moment, in the twinkling of an eye, at the last trumpet. For the trumpet will sound, and the dead will be raised imperishable, and we will be changed. For this imperishable body must put on imperishability, and this mortal body must put on immortality.

(1 Cor 15:35-53)

What Sort of Body in the Resurrection?

Starting from the thrust given by St. Paul, we can continue our reflection, using all the resources that philosophy, anthropology, and contemporary theology give us. How may we understand the reality of a "spiritual body," which seems to be a contradiction in terms, since common sense tells us that what is body is not spirit, and what is spirit is not body?

Let us firstly locate the term *body* historically. Materially situated in space, the body is the means in which and by which human beings receive and live their personal existence, by exercising their freedom and responsibilities to themselves, others, the world, and God. It is in and by their bodies that human beings enter into communication with others and with themselves; it is in and by their bodies that they love, suffer physically and morally, work, and experience joy and pleasure. Situated in time, the body of a human being becomes a history: "Our individual history is recapitulated in our body, as we live it and act it out."[1]

Thus understood, insofar as it is human, our body can be reduced to neither to physico-chemical elements or to an organic and biological reality; it is not a mere ensemble of animal reactions, even though it assumes into itself all these levels of natural existence and through them remains closely bound in solidarity with the world we experience.

The body, then, is we ourselves. We do not have a body; we are body. For the ancients, the soul-body duality was not seen as two, heterogeneous components of our being, but as two points of view from which the totality of our being could be regarded. The "flesh" in Johannine language articulates an understanding of human existence that is located in the concrete and the historical, with its fragility and vulnerability. It is in this sense that the "Word became flesh" and that the Apostles' Creed mentions "the resurrection of the body." It is the same for the soul, which considers the totality of a human being from the point of view of a life force and spiritual transcendence vis-à-vis the world. Even the understanding of Greek antiquity, which sees the soul as the form of the body, recognizes this unity. For, in fact, the relation-

---

1. E. Pousset, "La Resurrection," *Nouvelle revue théologique* (1969) 1032.

ship between these two principles is one which constitutes a single being. From this point of view, our body is already a spiritual body, one which thinks and speaks, and one which desires that which is beyond the created realm—God.

The doctrine of the resurrection of the body tells us, then, that human beings will be saved in the concrete conditions of their lives. Thus it affirms two things at one and the same time: it affirms our historic continuity with the past, on which our identities depend, while affirming our discontinuity with the past as well. This discontinuity is created through death in which our connection with our past physical existence is broken; a new link is then formed with a new and glorious body, a body freed from natural constraints. By the power of the Spirit of God, the body becomes spirit, while the spirit becomes an incorruptible body.

Are we able to gain a picture of a risen body? Strictly speaking, we are not, because such a body radically escapes the confines of our earthly representations. Yet we can make use of the apparitions of Jesus in order to ascertain certain characteristics. Without doubt, these apparitions do not present to us the glorious state of Christ's body, such as it is in the glory of the Father, but only the state in which the risen one made himself known to the disciples who were not yet risen. Here we find continuity and discontinuity: continuity, since the disciples "recognize" Jesus, the one with whom they had lived before his passion; they recognize him from his telling gestures, gestures which are particularly characteristic of his person, like the breaking of bread. They also recognize him by his word and his explanations of Scripture. Yet there is also a discontinuity: Jesus is now free from the constraints of time and space. He makes himself present at will and breaks through all physical forms of resistance and manifests a lordly sovereignty.

We are also able to think of privileged moments in our own lives, instants of grace in which our bodies seemed spiritualized by the richness of the experience of which they were the subject. These would include mystical experiences of the saints, intense moments of romantic love, and the joy evoked by sublime art and beauty.

Resurrection and Reincarnation

What is the doctrine of reincarnation which seems so seducing to many of our contemporaries today? It originates from such Eastern religions as Hinduism and Buddhism in which it serves as a doctrine of salvation. It seeks to respond to fundamental questions of humanity: what is the destiny of human beings? and, is there a justice which will prevail beyond all the injustices of this world? Moreover, it creates a fusion between the idea of retribution and that of reincarnation in which "the modality of the passage of one body to another is determined by one's former life. Reincarnation is based on the law and desire of *karma* (a form of predestination) to which it is tied. We must emphasize that reincarnation is inherent in the wheel of destiny. It is far from being a good in itself. Rather, it appears that the end is to be delivered from our previous lives; salvation or true freedom consists in escaping from them."[2] Thus, from good actions come good rebirths; from bad actions come painful rebirths in which we begin again at the foot of the ladder. Emphasizing a spirituality of detachment, such doctrines from the East find certain parallels in the West, such as in the Orphic and hermetic traditions of Pythagoras and Plato.

Since the nineteenth century in the West, diverse theosophical or anthropological esoterisms have developed. Reincarnation is viewed in all of these as a trial on the way to fulfillment, for it is an indispensable moment in the development of the self and of freedom. Moreover, these modern doctrines are often couched in a pseudo-scientism so as to give them a certain legitimacy.[3]

Why are these so seductive in the post-Christian West? It is paradoxical that in a time of doubt regarding life after death, and doubt in the resurrection, we find a "return of the religious," but in the form of doctrines which are entirely foreign to the dominant Christian tradition. In this state of things, an inadequate preaching on the part of the Church no doubt bears partial re-

---

2. P. Gisel, "Discours sur l'au-dela de la mort. La théologie mise au défi," in *Réincarnation, immortalité, résurrection* (Bruxelles: Éditions Universitaires Saint-Louis, 1988) 241.
3. Cf. D. Foucher, *Réincarnation ou Resurrection?*, Éditions de Montligeon, 1989.

sponsibility, especially by going along with the cultural tendency to avoid the topic of death. The Christian response to the problem of evil seemed at least deceiving. Our world thus found itself before an abyss which it tried to fill. The contemporary infatuation for the East determined that the search would move in the direction of reincarnation. For however unacceptable the answers given, one must recognize that positively, these Eastern doctrines do raise important questions: the spiritual question, eternal life, the desire for happiness and justice, the meaning of human existence, and the anguish at seeing one's life decided by a poorly made choice.

Where then is the incompatibility between these doctrines of reincarnation and Christianity? Reincarnation puts into jeopardy the unity of the person as a unique and irreplaceable subject before God. It falls into a certain dualism of body and soul, the first being finally without value, a simple dress, periodically replaced, and the second is reduced to a principle which changes its mode of being in every existence and whose final destiny is to lose itself in the great All. The unity and irreplaceable value of the person comes from the fact that each person works out their eternal destiny in an earthly existence which is unique, and that they are called to salvation in the totality of their person, body and soul. It is this which the Christian doctrine of the resurrection affirms, as opposed to the reincarnated being who is no longer conscious of what they have already lived, and who has thus lost their unity of being over the course of time.[4]

Jesus, when viewed through the lens of the reincarnation doctrine, takes on a whole new shape: resurrection becomes a reincarnation of a being, exceptional perhaps in sanctity, but who remains rigidly locked in the cycle of destiny. He appears like an "avatar," or one manifestation of the divine in the midst of others. The unique character of the mediator between God and human beings no longer exists.

Lastly, the doctrine of reincarnation articulates a movement from the human to God, a self-impelled movement which seeks to obtain salvation by human strength, to raise oneself up from

4. Cf. W. Kasper, "Réincarnation et christianisme," *Documentation catholique* 2005 (1990) 453–455, which expresses clearly why reincarnation is incompatible with Christianity.

step to step until one reaches *nirvâna* or supreme serenity; it is more through our struggle, as human beings, that we achieve perfection, than through our encounter with God. Christianity, on the contrary, proclaims the absolute priority of a God who seeks human beings, who goes to meet them in order to draw them to himself, a God who, in his mercy and love, wants to establish personal communion with human beings.

5

He Will Return in Glory
to Judge the Living and the Dead

The Return of Christ

The second article of the Creed, which contains the affirmations of faith in Christ, does not stop at the resurrection and ascension of Jesus; it proclaims his glorious return for the last judgment. In this it faithfully follows the message of the New Testament which clearly proclaims Christ's return, or his "parousia," a Greek term which means "presence" or "arrival": for the "Son of Man" will return (Matt 10:23; 16:25; 19:28, etc.). This return of Christ is described in the Gospels in the form of an apocalyptic scenario involving great tribulations and cosmic rumblings. These last convulsions of the sinful world will be preliminary signs. Then "the sign of the Son of Man will appear in heaven, and then all the tribes of the earth will mourn, and they will see 'the Son of Man coming on the clouds of heaven' with power and great glory" (Matt 24:30).

For Paul, too, this return of Christ will pass through a time of trials (1 Thess 5:3), but finally his definitive victory over his enemies will be sealed (1 Cor 15:24-28). This will also be the day of the resurrection of the dead and of our encounter with Christ: "For the Lord himself, with a cry of command, with the archangel's call and with the sound of God's trumpet, will descend from heaven, and the dead in Christ will rise first. Then we who are alive, who are left, will be caught up in the clouds together with them to meet the Lord in the air; and so we will be with the Lord forever" (1 Thess 4:16-17). In a completely different milieu, the angels will come to console the disciples who, after the ascension, continued to gaze into heaven: "This Jesus, who has been taken up from you into heaven, will come in the same way as you saw him go into heaven" (Acts 1:11). Revelation, which likes to define God as "The one who is, who was and who is to come" (Rev 1:4; 4:8; 11:17; 16:5), and which calls Jesus the Alpha and Omega (Rev 22:13), the beginning and the end, which is a properly divine attribute, ends on a note of longing which sums up the whole spirituality of the early Church Christians: "Amen, come Lord Jesus!" (Rev 22:20).

For the early Church apologists, the complementarity of the two comings of Christ is essential if one wants to properly understand Jesus' role as savior, and the way in which he fulfills the prophecies. Just as he came the first time "in suffering, without form or glory, crucified," says the Christian philosopher Justin in the second century, so he will return in glory, with eternal sovereignty and the full manifestation of his divine power, with which he will judge the world. This glory is that which he has already received from his Father through the resurrection and ascension. Thus, what is still hidden in our salvation, still unfinished, shall be totally accomplished. The "for us" of the resurrection shall be fully manifested.

There is a correspondence between the mystery of Christ and the lot of Christians who suffer today as Christ suffered, and who will reign with him as he reigns. Thus the confession of faith in Jesus is not only fixed on a past event; it also stretches toward the future in its hope of the second coming of the Lord.

Our Difficulties in the Face of this Message

The message of faith poses several difficulties to our contemporary mentality. First, the world of apocalyptic images is not one with which we are familiar; the cosmology and picture of the world that they suppose has been completely superceded by a scientific worldview; we think of such apocalyptic images as being part of a superstitious and mythological world of the past. On the other hand, we seek eagerly but in vain for bridges between the message of faith and what contemporary science might tell us about the end of the world. We need to remember what

---

We Shall Be Always with the Lord

But we do not want you to be uninformed, brothers and sisters, about those who have died, so that you may not grieve as others do who have no hope. For since we believe that Jesus died and rose again, even so, through Jesus, God will bring with him those who have died. For this we declare to you by the word of the Lord, that we who are alive, who are left until the coming of the Lord, will by no means precede those who have died. For the Lord himself, with a cry of command, with the archangel's call and with the sound of God's trumpet, will descend from heaven, and the dead in Christ shall rise first. Then we who are alive, who are left, will be caught up in the clouds together with them to meet the Lord in the air; and so we will be with the Lord forever. Therefore encourage one another with these words.

(1 Thess 4:13-18)

---

was said at the beginning of this book: the message of the end of time surpasses, by definition, all that we can imagine. It is necessary, therefore, to use images to describe what cannot be described. The language is a poetic, mythological one, not to be taken in a literal sense, as though it were a journalistic report of the future. Its aim is to give us a *sense,* a religious sense or meaning, of the end of time and of the world in regard to God and to Christ. It is this meaning that we must seek. Such language also puts us on guard against any sort of *concordism*[1] between science and faith, for scientific discourse about the origin and end of the world is of a completely different order. Thus we should avoid a too-easy concordance between religious representations, on the one hand, and the "journey of discovery" mode of modern science on the other.

Yet the difficulty continues. What is the meaning of these dramatic scenarios? And of what use are they for our faith? They

---

1. *Concordism* is the attempt to interpret biblical texts in a way that seeks to establish a synthesis between the images of the biblical account and scientific hypotheses about the origin and end of the world, so as to better defend the truth of Scripture. But the message of the Bible is not a teaching on the unfolding of phenomena, but a whole picture which seeks to express the relationship between God and human beings.

tell us, under the veil of images, that the mystery of the passion, death, and resurrection of Christ will be reproduced in an analagous way in the whole of his body which is the Church. All his life, Jesus confronted the powers of evil which fought against him. All the life of the Church is marked by the same battle, not only an exterior battle fought with powers outside the Church, but also an interior combat, for sin continues to be at work even in the Church. For "the pilgrim Church . . . bears the form of the time in which it lives; it lives among creatures who suffer and who are still at present undergoing the pangs of childbirth and waiting for the revelation of the sons [Ed: and daughters?] of God" (cf. Rom 8:22, 19) (Vatican II, *Lumen Gentium* 48). Jesus, of course, was the victim of this battle as it unleashed the powers of evil intent on his suffering and death. Such will also be the destiny of the Church, called to live through death in the cause of justice, which will be for it, as it was for Jesus, a passage to God. Such too is the Church's destiny in the death of each of its members and of all those who die for the cause of justice. Jesus knew, in the end, of his definitive resurrection; the Church, too, will know of its resurrection when the risen Lord returns to allow humanity to participate fully in his own life. The kingdom of God, inaugurated on earth, will thus expand to receive its total fulfillment from God (cf. *Lumen Gentium*). In other words, the event lived by Jesus is eschatological in that it both anticipates the end of time and prefigures it. Therefore, if we wish to contemplate both the end of time and our own end, we must consider the mystery of Christ.

But there is a historic difficulty with which we must deal: did not Jesus announce the end of time as something very imminent, an event to happen in his lifetime or shortly thereafter? Does not this apocalyptic discourse say, "Truly, I tell you, this generation will not pass away until all these things have taken place" (Matt 24:34-35)? Paul, too, evokes, in his scenario of the end of time, the case of those who will still be living when Christ returns. It seems that the first Christian generation lived in a climate of anticipation for an imminent end of time.

This fact is incontestable. In many of his eschatalogical discourses, Jesus articulates a vision of the end times: however, there is a verse in which he expresses his ultimate ignorance of the matter: "But about that day and hour no one knows, neither the angels of heaven, nor the Son, but only the Father" (Matt 24:36;

cf. Mark 13:32). If we can thus speak of a chronological error on the part of the primitive Christian community, such chronological urgency was the spontaneous expression of the felt urgency of salvation and conversion, an urgency created afresh by the simple fact of Jesus' presence. From this point of view, the time is short for us, as it was for the first Christians: it is urgent for us to be converted and believe. These discourses always include a call to vigilance: "Keep awake, therefore, for you do not know on what day your Lord is coming" (Matt 24:42). Another discursive strategy is to compare the end times to a thief. It is not difficult to see the relevance of such a call for our own lives.

"The Renewal of the Universe" (Matt 19:28)

The point of these images is also to tell us that Christ's return concerns not only humanity but the whole cosmos. The empty tomb was a discreet sign, given to faith, of the great eschatological rupture which must happen to the world which passes (1 Cor 7:31). The present world is destined to disappear (Rev 6:12-17; 20:11) or, more exactly, to be transformed into a new creation, fit for the "new creation" (Gal 6:15) of saved humanity. "For the creation waits with eager longing for the revealing of the children of God; for the creation was subjected to futility, not of its own will but by the will of the one who subjected it, in hope that the creation itself will be set free from its bondage to decay and will obtain the freedom of the glory of the children of God. We know that the whole of creation has been groaning in labor pains until now" (Rom 8:19-22). And that God's design is to recapitulate the whole creation in Christ, to "gather up all things in him, things in heaven and things on earth" (Eph 1:10, cf. Col 1:20). The creator of the universe will also be its eschatological "recreator." This is why the visionary of Revelation can proclaim: "Then I saw a new heaven and a new earth; for the first heaven and the first earth has passed away, and the sea was no more. . . . Death will be no more;/ mourning and crying and pain will be no more,/ for the first things have passed away" (Rev 21:1-4; cf. 2 Pet 3:13). Our present world, therefore, will be the site of the new, celestial Jerusalem, home of God with humanity, a home which includes our physical body in its individual, social, and cosmic form. No dimension of our being or action is excluded.

The Day of Judgment

Yet the day of the Lord's return will also be a day of judgment. The whole of the Old Testament bears witness to the Day of the Lord which is seen as a mighty intervention of God in the major events of Israel's history. These interventions are often described in apocalyptic images, for what will happen in history points toward the expectation of the last day, the day of final judgment, which will come to Israel as well as the other nations. With the coming of Jesus, the day of the Lord becomes the "day of our Lord Jesus Christ" (1 Cor 1:8). For God had given to his Son "authority to execute judgment, because he is the Son of Man" (John 5:27).

The Gospel of Matthew describes this scene in a solemn manner: "When the Son of Man comes in his glory, and all the angels with him, then he will sit on the throne of his glory. All the nations will be gathered before him, and he will separate people one from another as a shepherd separates the sheep from the goats. . ." (Matt 25:31-32). Each will be judged according to their charity toward the powerless, the hungry, the thirsty, strangers, the naked, the sick, and those in prison, with whom Jesus identifies himself. The criterion of judgment is that of loving gratitude on the part of Jesus and in all those for whom he died.

Announcing the day of judgment is also part of his apostolic preaching: "because he has fixed a day on which he will have the world judged in righteousness by a man whom he has appointed, and of this he has given assurance to all by raising him from the dead" says Paul in his discourse in the Areopagus at Athens (Acts 17:31; cf. 1 Pet 4:5; Heb 6:2). For it is Christ who will exercise the function of judge of the living and the dead (2 Tim 4:1). This judgment will cause fear and trembling for the impious, rebellious, and for unbelievers. His day will thus be a "day of wrath, when God's righteous judgment will be revealed" (Rom 2:5). It is worth noticing here a small difference in the language of Paul and John: for John, all the dead will rise—those who have done good to the resurrection as well as those who have done evil to the resurrection (cf. John 5:29). Paul, on the other hand, does not envisage a resurrection of the wicked because the resurrection is synonymous with life and salvation, and therefore only the just will rise.

How can we reconcile the image of God as judge with that of savior? For we are also told that "God did not send the Son into the world to condemn the world, but in order that the world might be saved through him" (John 3:17). The last judgment will not be the decision of a merciless judge with a taste for punishing all the weaknesses of human beings. This judgment will be founded on the judgment of condemnation of sin and of justification of the sinner, accomplished by the cross of Christ. For the justice of God is first of all a justice which saves, justifies, and sanctifies. There will only be a judgment of condemnation for those who have formally rejected the salvation offered by Jesus. This is why the judgment of the world began the moment the Father sent his Son; what is called the last judgment is only the full manifestation of what has already happened in human hearts. Condemnation, therefore, is done by ourselves: "Those who believe in him are not condemned; but those who do not believe are condemned already, because they have not believed in the name of the only Son of God" (John 3:18), and they refused the light. The point of this teaching is to remind us of the decisive and eternal consequences of our freedom in regard to God, and not to tell us who and how many shall be condemned.[2]

2. Cf. the later chapter dealing with the subject of hell, pp. 92–101.

When the Son of Man Comes in Glory . . .

When the Son of Man comes in his glory, and all the angels with him, then he will sit on the throne of his glory. All the nations will be gathered before him, and he will separate people one from another as a shepherd separates the sheep from the goats, and he will put the sheep at his right hand and the goats at the left. Then the king will say to those at the right hand, "Come, you that are blessed by my Father, inherit the kingdom prepared for you from the foundation of the world; for I was hungry and you gave me food, I was thirsty and you gave me something to drink, I was a stranger and you welcomed me, I was naked and you gave me clothing, I was sick and you took care of me, I was in prison and you visited me." Then the righteous will answer him, "Lord, when was it that we saw you hungry and gave you food, or thirsty and gave you something to drink?" . . . And the king will answer them, "Truly I tell you, just as you did it to one of the least of these who are members of my family, you did it to me." Then he will say to those at his left hand, "You that are accursed, depart from me into the eternal fire prepared for the devil and his angels; for I was hungry and you gave me no food, I was thirsty and you gave me nothing to drink. . . ." Then they will also answer, "Lord, when was it that we saw you hungry or thirsty or a stranger or naked or sick or in prison, and did not take care of you?" Then he will answer them, "Truly I tell you, just as you did not do it to one of the least of these, you did not do it to me." And these will go away into eternal punishment, but the righteous into eternal life.

(Matt 25:31-46)

PART II

The Christian
in the Face of Death
and the "Beyond"

6

Human Beings and Death

Before examining a Christian understanding of death, we shall first examine how we understand it individually—that is, psychologically—as well as look at cultural understandings of death. Of course no one can define for another the meaning of death; each of us has our own experience. On the other hand, our individual understanding and experience of death is significantly shaped by cultural understandings.

The Experience of Our Death

First, death can be considered as a universal biological event which comes to both the animal and vegetable species. The Bible gives an echo of this: "All people are grass,/ their constancy is like the flower of the field./ The grass withers, the flower fades" (Isa 40:6-7). In the third century Tertullian remarked that all that is born dies. But at death, as well as at birth, the living pay tribute to both, which serves as a symbolic affirmation of life. Throughout history, the learned have asked whether death is necessary, or what life might look like without the shadow of death looming large over it. In the end, however, all that can be said with certainty is that life is a cycle, and that cycle includes a variety of stages, including aging and death. Although in actuality very much a part of life, death appears to us as something intruding from the outside. Because of its enormity, however, most of us submit to it, that is, learn to incorporate our mortality into our psyches and identities.

In nature we know that all living beings are subject to death, yet human beings are the only animals who know that they are going to die. Because of our natural survival instinct, which death of course threatens, death weighs heavily upon our beings. Moreover, death calls into question all our creative work and earthly projects; therefore death appears as absurd or makes our lives appear as absurd, for such projects no longer make sense in the light of death. In addition, human beings fear the moral and physical suffering which often accompany death, whether the death be violent, sudden and unexpected, or at the end of an illness. In short, we are all inhabited by the anguish which death evokes in us.

However, history shows us that we possess an indomitable hope of conquering death. This manifests itself in diverse ways: of course to give one's life for a cause which goes beyond oneself is a way of giving meaning to our death and thus to our life; another form of overcoming death is to hope for immortality through spiritualities of reincarnation. The death of Socrates, who was unjustly condemned to death by poisoning, is one of the most noble examples of a serene, peaceful attitude in the face of death, an attitude full of hope in immortality.

The Death of Others

Death touches us through the death of others, in particular through the deaths of those who are dearest to us—parents, a spouse, children, friends, those with whom we work or with whom we suffer trials. Health professionals—doctors and nurses in hospitals and hospices—experience on a daily basis the death of those who have confided in them. In light of the death of loved ones, our suffering is twofold: first, we must witness attentively their act of dying, with all its trials and sufferings; then we must live through the anguish of separation from our beloved and the rupture of our affections for them.

To witness the death of a beloved is challenging, the intensity of which is proportionate to the intensity of our affections for them. In this sense, something of ourself dies, something without which, if deprived of completely, can make life seem unsustainable. Yet to witness the death of another is always a trial, whether we are close to that person or not, because such deaths harken us to our own death and our emotions associated with it. Thus numerous attitudes of flight or denial may surface. Today we are rediscovering how important it is to give the dying attention and love in a self-forgetting, generous way. Of course our presence is critical for the dying person; however our presence to them will most likely have a transforming effect upon us as well.

As death comes, we undergo a gradual separation with the dying, which we experience in several stages. In the beginning, as the dying person loses consciousness, we lose our ability to communicate with them. As this happens, we lose our sense of who they are; the dying person is no longer the "him" or "her" we once knew, only an empty shell. Of course, this experience of the "empty shell" is all the more harsh for us if the dying is young or a child.

And Human Beings Go to Their Eternal Home . . .

Remember your creator in the days of your youth, before the days of trouble came, and the years draw near when you will say, "I have no pleasure in them"; before the sun and the light and the moon and the stars are darkened and the clouds return with the rain; in the day when the guards of the house tremble, and the strong men are bent, and the women who grind cease working because they are few, and those who look through the windows see dimly; when the doors to the street are shut, and the sound of the grinding is low, and one rises up at the sound of the bird, and all the daughters of song are brought low; when one is afraid of heights, and terrors are in the road; the almond tree blossoms, the grasshopper drags itself along and desire fails; because all must go to their eternal home, and mourners will go about the streets; before the silver cord is snapped, and the golden bowl is broken, and the pitcher is broken at the fountain, and the wheel broke at the cistern, and the dust returns to the earth as it was, and the breath returns to God who gave it. Vanity of vanities, says the Teacher; all is vanity.

(Eccl 12:1-8)

The Social Perception of Death

"Human beings have been sovereign masters and mistresses of their death and its circumstances for centuries. Today they are masters and mistresses no longer, and here is why. . . ." As Philippe Ariès[1] has written, death was regarded as part of a cycle of life and therefore was normal. Thus the dying realized their situation and adopted the necessary attitudes; if not, those around them felt duty bound to warn them. People sought, at whatever cost, to avoid a situation in which those who were dying were "deprived of their death"—that one must "live" their death. Death was viewed as a public event which, for some, took place in a "chamber of the dying" in which all those concerned—family members, neighbors—grieved and comforted the dying.[2] This was a place in which farewells were said, reconciliation between God and neighbor took place, and last wishes were made.

This approach to death has been almost completely superseded in the space of a few generations in which our contemporary practice opposes, almost point for point, the traditional norm. Doctors and their assistants generally consider it their duty to hide the fact of imminent death from the patient. It was this practice and understanding of death that Anne Philipe recounted in her moving book, *Le temps d'un soupir* (Julliard, 1963); in the same spirit, Simone de Beauvoir describes the last moments of her mother's life in *Une mort très douce* (Gallimard, 1964). How many times has one heard, as though it were a consolation, "They didn't realize they were dying," an expression which replaced the "feeling their death was near," of the seventeenth century.[3] Everything is organized so that human beings are deprived of their own death.

This is why people generally flee from death and its approach. Those dying or in agony come under the custodial care of the state in which they are hidden away in hospitals and hospices. They are condemned to live in fearful isolation, in the solitude inherent in death.

This law or taboo about death is imposed on dying people themselves, who are often quite aware of their state, but who find themselves forbidden to talk about it so as not to traumatize those

1. P. Ariès, "La mort inversée," *La Maison-Dieu,* 101 (1970) 59.
2. Ibid., 61.
3. Ibid., 63.

around them. "In former times, death was a tragedy—often a comic tragedy—where one played to those who were about to die. Today, death is a comedy—always a dramatic comedy—where one plays to those who do not know they are going to die."[4]

One can legitimately speak of a "denial of death" which continues after the death itself. Traditionally, death was seen as such a weighty event that there was no need for social and religious symbolization through rites which try to express its meaning, not only in terms of respect for the dead but also attempting to express the encounter of the group with a mysterious transcendence. This was done through funerals, eulogies, mourning clothes and signs, condolences, memorial stones and plaques, and cemeteries. Through these rites the "work of grieving" is carried out; that is to say, our relationship to the deceased is transformed. The links to the deceased become untied and give way to other links.

But in recent decades one has seen a massive disaffection regarding funeral rites, sometimes even their rejection or prohibition. The scattering of ashes after certain cremations is one example of this in that it eliminated all trace of the dead person; after this scattering no inscription keeps alive their name. "Death praxis" in Anglo-Saxon countries is an even graver symptom of this attitude, where commercial enterprises treat and make up the human remains in order to give them the appearance of being alive, and display them in an armchair, cigarette in hand. Thus even the image of someone lying down, a symbol of the dead, is rejected. One can conclude, perhaps with a certain exaggeration, that this denial is radical, universal (at the level of statistics), culturally passed on, and pathogenic—that is, the generator of a new form of anguish.[5] Thus because death is denied, we can act as though it does not exist.

We live in a time of deep anxiety regarding death, and thus seek to hide from it, and hide it from us. Yet our struggle with the idea of death now surfaces in a new and unique way: in violent death as portrayed in film and television, in car accidents, or in pursuit of high-risk sporting activities such as mountain climbing, river rafting, sky diving, and hang gliding. This incongruence is not inexplicable, as it expresses the contradiction in

4. Ibid., 64.
5. Cf. P. Druet, *Pour vivre sa mort,* Le Sycomore, 57–58.

attitudes embodied by human beings regarding death, an attitude that is unable to make sense of death. And if death no longer has meaning, it should come as no surprise that life no longer has meaning either; this reality is expressed in a variety of ways, but most notably through risky behavior and lifestyles and the high suicide rate, especially among the young.

Today, however, there are many signs that this "culture of death" is at an impasse; it has exacted too much unjust pain and suffering on too many innocent people. We are increasingly seeing among many doctors and hospitals a new attitude developing regarding those who may no longer be restored to health. For example, accompanying of the sick and the dying is increasingly viewed as an essential task; specialized services of palliative care are developing wherein doctors are accompanied by psychologists and volunteers, all of whom are more willing to work in liaison with priests and pastors. Death is becoming again the locus of a sharing of gifts. It is becoming a moment in which a major question is asked: What is a human being?

As with the dying, those in mourning are increasingly receiving attention and assistance from civil and private organizations to help facilitate their role in death. These evolving attitudes toward death are also valuing the importance of funeral rites, especially for their role in facilitating the "work of grieving" for the bereaved. Likewise, funeral rites are attempting to incorporate new insights regarding death by providing for the bereaved someone who has already experienced loss by the death of a close one. However, the approach of this assistance provided by churches is not only therapeutic; it is spiritual as well as it recognizes the need to engage the whole person with the loss of a loved one through death.

In recent years there has also been a growing interest in "frontier" experiences of death. Several books have studied these from a scientific point of view. It is striking that independent accounts tell a relatively consistent story (feelings of peace and serenity, going through a tunnel, out of body experience or bilocation of the person, perception of a being of light, panorama of life, etc.). These factors are at one with certain psychological and spiritual/literary testimonies (*Bede the Venerable*; the *Dream of Gerontius* by J. H. Newman). The most consistent message is that those who have a near-death experience often declare that they can no longer live as before, that their attitude in the face of death has been profoundly changed.

Such testimonies of near-death experience should be welcomed and respected. At the same time it should be said that the language used to describe such experiences often attempts to say something about that which is "beyond" life.[6] However, this is not quite the case. That which was understood and described as "clinical death" was often, in fact, an "apparent death"—that is, a psychic or spiritual experience, but not an actual experience of death and then returning to life. We know this as there are many similar experiences described by people who experienced them in contexts unrelated to death. Because such descriptions, then, are not of the "beyond as such," we must avoid making connections between such "ethereal bodies" and the nature of the spiritual bodies of which faith speaks. The world and language of faith envisages an order which wholly transcends the conditions of our time and space, while our descriptions remain in the domain of sensual experience.

---

6. I regret that the titles of Dr. Raymond Moody's bestsellers, *Life After Death* (Harrisburg: Stackpole, 1976) and *New Light on Life After Death*, increases this confusion. The author himself, whose honesty and modesty in his research should not be doubted, and who refuses to see in the experiences he recounts a scientific "proof" of a life after death, is wrong nevertheless to speak as though clinical death is real death, and thus as though these accounts report a first experience of the "beyond." On this subject, while remaining sympathetic to Dr. Moody's book, one may profitably consider the point made by H. Küng in *Eternal Life* (New York: Doubleday, 1984).

7

To Die in Christ

The enigma of death poses a grave question to Christian faith. For death is both a place of horror and rejection, as well as a place of hope. Why death? Who made death? To what does death lead, since we see it only, as it were, from behind, through those who depart? Is it an absolute end, a fall into nothingness, or a departure and passage toward another life? What connection can we maintain with the departed? Must we speak of them as the "dead" or, on the contrary, as the "living"?

God Did Not Make Death

Why death? From where does death come? Why did God, who is described as good, create human beings destined for death? Scripture's reply to this question is formal: ". . . God did not make death, and he does not delight in the death of the living" (Wis 1:13). Christianity is not a religion of death. But how then does it seem to us that death is a law of nature?

The reply is also clear, and it sends us to the first pages of Genesis[1] in which God says to Adam, "But of the tree of the knowledge of good and evil you shall not eat, for in the day you eat of it you shall die" (Gen 2:17). This warning does not announce a punishment, properly speaking, but the inevitable con-

1. Most today accept that the accounts of the creation and fall in the book of Genesis are not literal accounts of events based on eyewitness reports, but stories (of mythical nature, a term here used positively) whose aim is to give a revealed religious teaching and to account for the present state of humanity by creating a story of its origin.

sequence of a decision which sought to take by force what could only be known as a gift. Death, as addressed here, is both a spiritual and physical death. For human beings, now separated from God and no longer living in his Spirit, lose the equilibrium and solidity of their being and become fragile, a fragility which ends in death. This degradation was produced in the scene of the temptation, at the end of which God says to human beings: "By the sweat of your face you shall eat bread/ until you return to the ground, for out of it you were taken;/ you are dust/ and to dust you shall return" (Gen 3:19). The book of Wisdom comments, ". . . but through the devil's envy death entered the world" (Wis 2:24). This judgment is elaborated by St. Paul: "Therefore, just as sin came into the world through one man, and death came through sin, and so death spread to all because all have sinned . . ." (Rom 5:12).

Therefore we must look behind the figurative language of the Bible if we are to find that death—as we experience it, with all the anguish and suffering it brings—does not belong to the creative intention of God. Death is the result of humanity's inclination toward sin: Death is the consequence of the temptation and sin of humanity. The death which we experience is the result of a disorder introduced into our relationship with the world and with nature by human sin, that is to say, by the initial rejection of God's gift.

"For the wages of sin is death," writes Paul (Rom 6:23). Christian revelation depicts physical death as both the sign (or the symptom) and the consequence of another, interior death, which consists in the separation of human beings from God. Likewise, our human equilibrium is found in our communion with God, which includes a vocation to immortality and incorruptibility. When this communion ceases, we are deprived of something very central to our being, without which we are now subject to death. On the other hand, as scripture emphasizes, eternal life is offered to us in Jesus Christ our Savior.

What Is Death?

In the light of the above, can we express more clearly the nature of death? Death is not an absolute end in and of itself; rather death remains the journey toward eternity. Because of sin, however, this journey must be made on the road of suffering, a road that takes us from the world to another realm within. But this is no safe passage, for those who have the misfortune to undertake such a journey in the state of sin, eternal death will be their destiny; but for those who journey in the company of Christ's salvation, eternal life in God will be their destiny. Thus, when we speak of "the dead," we must mean those who have experienced the "second death" (Rev 20:6)—that is, those who die a definitive death without the benefit of the resurrection. In contrast to the definitively dead, there are those who have "passed away," that is those who are in reality alive—alive in God.

Traditional Church teaching maintains that death is the separation of body and soul. This doctrine is increasingly difficult for us to accept, however, for our modern emphasis is on the essential unity of body and soul: today, maintaining the existence of one without the other is difficult. Properly understood, however, the soul is the form of the person which endures after the body has disintegrated. The soul is understood here "in the biblical sense of the word, not as a part of the human being alongside the body, but as the vital principle of a human being, considered in their unity and their totality, in other words, their 'me,' the center of their person."[2] Definitively, the separation of body and soul signifies that the departed remain living beings.

Since the soul is that which animates the human person, and since the body is the person in relationship to the world, the two cannot be completely separated. "In death," writes Rahner, "the soul does not become acosmic, but if we may so express it, pancosmic,"[3] that is to say, far from being deprived of all ties with our world, it communicates with it in a more open, universal way. This reality remains unimaginable for us because we are not yet risen, but it belongs to the domain of resurrection.

2. *La foi de l'Église* (Paris: Cerf, 1987) 395.
3. K. Rahner, *Le chrétien et la mort* (Foi vivante, 1966) 22.

"O my God, grant that after having discovered the joy of utilizing every growth for making you grow in me, I may come to that last phase of communion in which I possess you in accepting to diminish in you.

"Grant that, my hour having come, I may recognize you under the form of each strange hostile power or enemy which seems to want to destroy or supplant me. When age begins to mark my body (and even more my spirit); when the evil which lessens me or carries me off weighs on me from within; at the sorrowful moment when suddenly I realize that I am ill or that I have become old, and especially at that last moment when I feel that I am passive, no longer able to control my being, and in the hands of the great unknown forces which formed me, in all these somber hours, allow me, my God, to understand that it is you (providing that my faith is great enough) who painfully pulls apart the fibers of my being right to the marrow of my substance, in order to carry me off into you.

"Yes, the more the future opens before me as a vertiginous crevasse or an obscure passage, the more, if I dare to venture forward in trust, on the strength of your word, am I able to lose myself or lower myself in you, to be assimilated by your body Jesus!

"O Energy of my Lord, irresistible, living force, because of we too, you are the strongest, infinitely so, the task of burning me up in the union which must solder us together is yours. . . .

"It is not enough that I die in communicating. . . . Teach me to communicate in dying."

Pierre Teilhard de Chardin, prayer cited by P. D'Ouince in his allocution in the chapel at the rue de Sèvres, April 27, 1955. Cf. H. de Lubac, *La pensée religieuse du P. Teilhard de Chardin* (Aubier: 1973) 373-74.

To Die in Christ

For human beings death is not only a passion to undergo but an act to accomplish. Human beings are given a fundamental choice: to live in freedom by opting for that which is eternal, or to build upon that which is temporal and passes with death. Our option to build upon that which is eternal is scaled in our death: that is, the meaning we give to our death is consistent with the meaning we gave to our lives. In this sense, death can have meaning for us.

Because of the salvation brought by the death and resurrection of Christ, all human beings are offered the opportunity to die in Christ so as to rise with him. Christ, by his victory over death, has changed death's meaning. In regard to our solidarity with Adam, death is the price we pay for sin; in regard to our solidarity with Christ, death becomes a saving event.

Just as Christ called his own death a baptism, Paul understands baptism as an entry into, and a participation in, the mystery of the death and resurrection of Christ (cf. Rom 6:2-11). During our earthly life Jesus' death and resurrection are already a reality, which develops throughout our life: "Always carrying in the body the death of Jesus, so that the life of Jesus may also be made visible in our bodies. For while we live, we are always being given up to death for Jesus' sake, so that the life of Jesus may be made visible in our mortal flesh" (2 Cor 4:10-12). However, death and life include future: ". . . for you have died and your life is hidden with Christ in God. When Christ who is your life is revealed, then you also will be revealed with him in glory" (Col 3:3). Death is the ultimate accomplishment and the supreme ratification of our baptism, the fullness of our death to sin and entry into the resurrection of Christ. This is why Paul is wholly stretched toward the future in the desire to know Christ: "if somehow I may attain the resurrection from the dead" (Phil 3:11). He even says, "For to me, living is Christ and dying is gain . . . my desire to depart and be with Christ, for that is far better" (Phil 1:21-24). It is thus that Stephen dies, imitating Christ's death (Acts 7:59-60). So, too, Ignatius of Antioch said that he would only be truly Christian after having been "ground" like wheat by the beasts. Such is the testimony of the saints, ancient and modern.

Christians are thus called to make of their death a gift of themselves to God "completing what is lacking in Christ's afflictions for the sake of his body, that is, the church" (Col 1:24), and to give the greatest proof of love in giving their lives for their friends. To help us in this, the Church offers three sacraments which reproduce in some sense the three sacraments of Christian initiation under the form of a new initiation into life in the glory of God: the sacrament of reconciliation actualizes the grace of baptism; the anointing of the sick is a new confirmation, a gift of the strength of the Holy Spirit in times of illness and crisis; a travelling allowance in our journey from Christ at baptism to Christ at death.

8

Between Two Resurrections

The Thorny Question of the "Between Time"—
Between Death and Final Resurrection

What happens to those beloved beings that we have seen die?
What will be our own lot after death? These urgent questions live
within us and we often feel frustrated before the proposed
responses. Yet there is a good and bad curiosity, the word of the
Church will never satisfy the second kind.

In the first part of this book, I examined the resurrection of
the dead and the last judgment. But that was from a universal
perspective concerning the end of the time to come. The question now posed concerns each one of us as individuals. The question is, of course, posed in temporal terms because we still live
in time: What is the condition of those who have left us in the
"between time" which separates their bodily death and their final
resurrection?

We know the response of the classic catechism: appearing before God, the deceased are judged by the fundamental orientation they gave to their lives. If they are saved, their souls alone
are admitted, after the necessary purifications, to the vision of
God, while their bodies, which disintegrate in the tomb, must wait
for the return of Christ when they will be raised.

But this vision has become ever more difficult for contemporary sensitivities: the condition of being a "soul separated from
its body" appears contradictory to our human condition, to which
the fact of being body is essential. Disembodied, our being appears evanescent and deprived of concrete personality—of its

"ME." We have difficulty thinking of a blessed life in terms of a soul without its body.

Yet if we say, responding to our deepest desire, that those who have left us are already risen, we fall too into other difficulties: we make light of the fundamental experience of separation between them and us, of the dissolution of bodies in tombs, and we also risk thinking of a resurrection which would be in total discontinuity with the experience of earthly life. The separation between our world and the world of glory would be complete. Moreover, would not our conception of resurrection be too exclusively spiritual? At the same time, would we not reduce to insignificance the value of history which continues?

Are we not caught up on a wheel? When will the resurrection happen? The answer to this question is to be found in a paradox: we must say both that the dead are raised and that they are not yet raised. In other words, they live a first, incomplete resurrection, which will remain while the whole of humanity and the cosmos with it has not yet arrived at the full resurrection which will take place with Christ's return. The resurrection is not only a slow development, but also a dynamic process which develops between Jesus' resurrection on Easter morning and his second coming in glory at the end of time. Just as John in the book of Revelation speaks of the process that leads from the first to the second resurrection, so we may speak, in a very different sense, of the dynamic which leads from the first to the second resurrection.

Of this paradox the mystery of Jesus himself can give us an idea. He too knew an intermediate time when his body rested in the tomb, even if this body did not know decomposition. From the instant of his death on the cross, Jesus, perfectly holy and without any sin, was admitted in his humanity to the blessed vision of the Father. It concerned his concrete person, that of the Son as a human being, and not simply his "separated" human soul. For his Father and for him the instant of his death already coincided with that of his resurrection. As we have seen,[1] the ancient tradition of the Church has interpreted Christ's descent to the underworld as the inauguration of his resurrection.

---

1. Cf. ch. 3, "He descended into the underworld."

However, the resurrection of Jesus was not complete while the concrete sign of his bodily resurrection was not given to us. The event of Easter is the glorious fulfillment and total manifestation in his person of that first resurrection. Thanks to this event Jesus renews contact and communication with his friends and disciples through apparitions; he completes the founding of his Church and makes the economy of the sacraments possible, which supposes a contact between his glorified body and our still mortal bodies.

From the point of the divine eternity, we may well say that the two states are one. But from the fact of the incarnation, God enters into concrete relation with the temporal cycle. The distance between Jesus' death and resurrection also has a real value which is so much greater in that it embodies a parable in which we are told what we need to live.

The same affirmation may be made in regard to reflection on the "total Christ," that is to say, Christ who progressively unites humanity in order to make the Church his own Body. On the personal level, Christ is completely risen at Easter, inaugurating in his own person the end of time. But the process of resurrection that he has inscribed in humanity still continues. Until his return, his parousia, the total Christ is not completely resurrected because his resurrection has not yet transformed the cosmos and because those called to become his Body have not yet all become a body of risen people. His manifestation in glory is still postponed until the definitive accomplishment of his Pasch. The total Christ is both already and not yet risen.

What Is Particular Judgment?

We know that the great judgment of the world already began with the coming of Christ, and that judgment will be determined by our faith or our rejection of faith. Death is the moment when the orientation we have given our lives is sealed definitively. It is also the moment when God's judgment of us is definitive, when we find ourselves enjoying the light of God's salvation, or the darkness of our sin and death.

There is no doubt that Scripture prefers to talk of a general judgment. There is also a fundamental unity between general and particular judgment, through the tension of the "already here" and the "not yet." But the parable of Lazarus and the Rich Man gives us an indication of the reality of a judgment which takes place after death: "The poor man died and was carried away by the angels to be with Abraham. The rich man also died and was buried. In hades, where he was being tormented, he looked up and saw Abraham far away with Lazarus by his side" (Luke 16:22-23).

The First Resurrection

The language of the New Testament speaks of life and even of resurrection, without necessarily speaking of general resurrection, for the promise of life eternal is linked to Christ's resurrection and is accessible by each human person. Jesus says to the good thief: "Truly, I tell you, today you will be with me in Paradise" (Luke 23:43). The "you" of the good thief will be with the *me* of Jesus. In one case as in the other, it involves a concrete person, the living subject of their own "I." Also, the *today* is to be taken seriously as it expresses the immediacy of salvation. There is no such thing here as a separated soul.

We may also look at Jesus' dialogue with Martha, Lazarus' sister. At Jesus' word, "your brother will rise again," Martha responds with all the force of her Jewish faith: "I know he will rise on the last day." But Jesus invites her to make a new act of faith in him, the source of a life which is already present: "I am the resurrection and the life. Those who believe in me, even though they die, will live and never die" (John 11:25-26). Faith in Jesus is thus a force of life capable of conquering death, for even those who experience physical death remain alive.

Paul does not hesitate to speak, as we have seen, of a resurrection already accomplished in the grace of baptism.[2] If the economy of grace already includes a participation in Christ's resurrection, how much more the economy of glory will include the elect, even before its total fulfillment! Just as our life is hidden with Christ in God (cf. Col 3:3), so the lives of the elect remain hidden in God.

There was an element of hesitation on the part of the Church in terms of its theological reflection on the mystery of the resur-

2. Cf. ch. 3, "He is risen for us."

rection. This hesitation is due to the tension between the collective resurrection of all the faithful at the end of time and the question of individuals who have died before the end of time. This was understandable as biblical references were generally concerned with the final resurrection; moreover, it proved difficult to speak of resurrection of bodies with disintegrating corpses still in the tomb. To solve this tension, elements in the Church argued that this time "in between the times" be viewed as one of hibernation of bodies in winter, before the spring of resurrection. This solution was never officially accepted by the Church, yet it is a conventional wisdom to which many of the faithful subscribe. This is probably because, as with most errors, there is an element of truth to it.

In 1336, reacting against this theory, Pope Benedict XII taught that the "face to face" beatific vision of God by the saints is immediate, even "before the resurrection of their bodies and the general judgment." He also taught that, "By this vision and delight, the souls of those already dead are truly blessed and possess life and eternal rest. . . . Such a vision and such rejoicing in the divine essence causes acts of faith and hope to disappear in these souls."[3] Benedict's text is written in the context of the classic distinction between soul and body, and it reserves the term "resurrection" for the end of time. However, his main argument is that there is an immediate beatific life given to the *believing subject,* which is so great that there is no object left for the practice of faith and hope, for faith and hope have now become one in this beatitude. Is such happiness possible for a soul completely separated from its body? St. Thomas thinks that the perfect beatitude of human beings depends on both the soul and the body.[4]

Yet, as we have seen above,[5] "soul" in Benedict's statement must be understood in the biblical sense of the word: "In regard to faith, body and soul cannot be totally separated from each other, to the point that there is absolutely no link between them. It must be admitted that, after death, a certain relation to the body

---

3. G. Dumeige, *La foi catholique,* Orante, no. 962–64.
4. St. Thomas Aquinas, *Summa Theologica,* IIIa Q. 15. a. 10. c; cf. Ia, IIae Q. 4. a 5, 6.
5. Cf. ch. 7, "What is death?"

and to the world continues, an incomplete relation which is outside our experience."[6] The concern on the part of the Church here is in regard to the life of the just in God before the end of time. These teachings seek to avoid associating the resurrection with the Greek notion of the immortality of the soul, such as was taught by Plato. In contrast, a Christian understanding of the resurrection is one of a concrete person in God. As Irenaeus of Lyons writes:

> The soul and spirit may well be a part of the human being, but never the whole human being: the perfect human being is the mixture and the union of the soul which has received the Spirit of the Father and which has been mixed with the body fashioned according to the image of God. . . . For if one puts aside the substance of the body, that is to say, the fashioned creation, in order to consider what is properly spirit, such a thing is no longer a spiritual human being. . . . The soul alone is not a human being: it is only the soul of a human being and thus a part of the human being. Nor is the Spirit a human being: the Spirit is named Spirit, not human being. It is the mixture and the union of all these which constitutes a perfect human being.[7]

According to the logic of this text, one cannot therefore speak of the life of human beings in God without their bodies being involved in one way or another.

The life of the just in God is therefore already, in an incomplete and non-manifested way, a resurrection of the body. Besides this, the bodily and fully risen humanity of Christ exercises an eternal mediation for our access to the blessed vision of God. For how could it assume such a mediation vis-à-vis "separated" souls?[8]

6. *La Foi de l'Eglise,* 396.

7. Irenaeus of Lyons, *Against the Heresies,* trans. D. J. Unger (New York: Paulist, 1992) 6:33.

8. Cf. the same position taken by G. Greshake, *Plus fort que la mort* (Paris, 1978) and more recently, G. Greshake and J. Kremer, *Resurrectio mortuorum. Zum theologischen Verständnis der leiblichen Auferstehung* (Darmstadt: Wissenschaftliche Buchgesellschaft, 1986).

The Happiness of "Souls" in Heaven

Since the passion and death of our Lord Jesus Christ, they have seen and see the divine essence in an intuitive vision and even face to face, without the mediation of any creature as the object of vision. The divine essence rather manifests itself to them nakedly, clearly and openly (nude, clare ac aperte), *and by this vision they delight in this same essence. By this vision and this delight, the souls of those who are already dead are truly blessed and possess life and eternal rest. The souls of those who will die later will see this divine essence and will delight in it before the general judgment.*

Such a vision and such a delight in the divine essence make acts of faith and hope disappear in these souls, faith and hope being properly theological virtues. In addition, after such an intuitive face-to-face vision and such delight had begun, this same intuitive face-to-face vision and this same delight have continued, and will continue without interruption, until the last judgment, and, from there, forever.

(Benedict XII, Constitution *Benedictus Deus,* January 29, 1336)

The Second Resurrection

However, this resurrection is not yet complete by reason of human solidarity with each other, time and space, and with the cosmos. An incontestable sign is given to us regarding this incompletion: the decomposition of bodies in the tomb and the fact that God's elect can no longer communicate normally with us. This is why Scripture proclaims to us the general resurrection at the end of time, about which we spoke above.[9] For as long as human beings continue their difficult and painful earthly pilgrimage, and have not yet passed to the side of the resurrection, while the new heavens and new earth have not yet transformed the creation, while the risen Christ has not yet come to manifest his glory among human beings, the general resurrection remains in its genesis. The distinction between the first and second resurrections is that of something that passes from being unfinished, to its completion, or something which is hidden transformed by becoming manifest.

---

9. Cf. ch. 3 on the resurrection of Christ, pp. 23–30.

But, it may be asked, if God is eternal, is this way of distinguishing between the first and second resurrection too dependent upon temporal images? Could it not be that our death simply puts us at the end of time? Does not the general end of time correspond to the end of time for each of us? In other words, is there a need for the distinction between an immediate and a general resurrection? Is there a need for a doctrine of a time in between times?

This idea contains many elements of truth. We must not forget that the end of time is not merely a chronological event, but also a divine, transcendent, and already present event in which we now live. Moreover, Scripture itself tells us that the resurrection of Christ at the end of time has already arrived.

However, this view cannot be held exclusively without devaluing the importance of this world, of human history, which continues in the hope of the resurrection. The resurrection represents a promise which involves our fragile bodies which will eventually be raised.

From God's side, this view forgets that the divine eternity is so much eternity that it is capable of assuming the reality of time into itself, transcending, while respecting, it at one and the same time. In freely creating the world and, with it, time, God has already put himself in a relationship with time which he embraces as a unity. In addition, with the incarnation of the Son, God submitted himself to the law of time and remains, even in the resurrection of Jesus, the one who is subject to time. For, the event of Christ has a past, a present, and a future. Of course, these three instances of time are perpetually present to God's eternity. However, each keeps its value in God's eyes. It is the same for the salvation of humanity accomplished by the historical event of Christ. By virtue of a free initiation on his part, and through pure love, God mysteriously assumes into himself the tension between the "already" and the "not yet." Likewise, it is correct to say that the total Christ is not yet risen, as long as the world lasts. Neither can the resurrection of each be total, nor the resurrection of all be accomplished, until the end of time.

This distinction between the already and the not yet allows us to be aware of the difference between Jesus' resurrection and the resurrection for other human beings. On the other hand, the assumption of Jesus and Mary anticipates and foretells our own resurrection.

9

Heaven:
The Kingdom of God Fulfilled

Heaven, God's Dwelling

It is evident that the term *heaven,* as it is used here, does not designate a cosmic space where stars revolve on their course. From faith's point of view, this "heaven" is a physical and material reality. One must not, therefore, be surprised that Gagarin did not encounter God there. Our earth itself is an element of this heaven.

Yet the fathomless immensity of the sky and its being above us confers on it a symbolic value. "Heaven" expresses all that is beyond limit, and "above" not only what dominates us, but also what is good and noble. On the contrary, "below" designates what is evil, for example, the underworld or hell. The attribution of positive and negative values are conditioned by the upright posture of the human body and by the innate desire in the human heart to "grow up" and to "climb," as attested in the Bible by the mythic pride of the tower of Babel, and today, for example, by the desire to conquer not only the heaven of our earthly atmosphere (aviation), but also interastral space (orbital space stations, journeys to the moon).

The language of religion has spontaneously placed God above, in a symbolic representation of a "place" absolutely different from the places on earth. Both the Old and New Testaments use such an image: they envisage a world situated "above the earth," a superior zone comprising several levels (cf. Paul's "third heaven," 2 Cor 12:2) which lead to the most elevated level, that which is properly God's dwelling place. "Heaven" even serves as a metaphor to designate God himself. For example, Matthew speaks of the "kingdom of heaven" to say "kingdom of God." Jesus teaches us to pray saying, "Our Father in heaven" (Acts 1:10), that is to say, he rejoins his Father in glory, to sit at his right "in the heavens."

Heaven is also the "place" wherein those who are saved dwell: the "paradise" of human beings with God, situated in heaven, in the dwelling place of God. From this perspective heaven is not simply an "above" but also a "before"; it is that toward which we journey, that which will be the full realization of God as all in all. This is why Paul invites us to seek what is "above" (Col 3:1), where our true homeland is to be found (Phil 3:20).

Thus in the realm of faith, "heaven" is a metaphor which designates the fullness of salvation for human beings, that which is risen and passed into God. Should we continue to call it a *place?* Is it not more profoundly a "state" of human beings with God which cannot be localized anywhere? Fundamentally, yes. In this sense heaven is a "no-place," for it has no common measure with our space and with our time. However, this must not make us forget that salvation is concerned with the totality of the cosmos, including "matter" itself, even if any clear notion of the risen world is absolutely beyond us.

The Kingdom of God Inaugurated by the Resurrection of Christ

From the point of view of our salvation, heaven is based on the victory of Christ over death and his glorification with the Father in his risen body. In and through Christ, humanity inaugurates its definitive salvation. He is the head of the body which must rejoin him in order to share fully his filial relationship with the Father.

To those who might be tempted to consider talk of the Christian notion of heaven as a dangerous projection of the illusory desires of human beings, it must be said again that the glorious risen one remains in heaven the crucified one. He is the "slain Lamb" (Rev 5:12), "like that of a lamb without defect or blemish. He was destined before the foundation of the world, but was revealed at the end of the ages for your sake" (1 Pet 1:19-20).

In heaven remain Christ's glorious wounds as well as those of all humanity, now converted into acts of love.

If human beings have been created in the image and likeness of God, that is to say, in the image of Christ who is himself "the image of the invisible God" (Col 1:15), it is because the vocation to filial communion with the Father is deeply implanted in our being. This vocation can only be realized in and through Christ the eternal Son who became a human being in order to become our brother. Christ, through his paschal mystery, is the unique mediator between God and human beings in the accomplishment of our salvation; because his incarnation has made him a real human being for eternity, he remains forever the mediator of our communion with God. "In order that he might be the firstborn within a large family" (Rom 8:29), he makes us participate in his Spirit, which makes us cry "Abba! Father" (Rom 8:15). Temples of the Spirit, sisters and brothers of the Son and sons and daughters of the Father, those who have already shared in the Trinitarian life here on earth, will experience its full manifestation in glory.

As long as salvation is not totally accomplished and as long as the world and history continue, heaven will be "a greatness in growth," says Karl Rahner. Salvation will be perfectly realized with the accomplishment of all things at Christ's return, his judgment, and the general resurrection of all.

True Happiness: The True Life of Human Beings Is to See God

The fullness of life to which we aspire cannot be realized except in the vision of God, that is to say, in a loving knowledge which is the source of total happiness. Those with pure hearts will see God (cf. Matt 5:8). "And this is eternal life, that they may know you, the only True God, and Jesus Christ whom you have sent" (John 17:3). And "Beloved, we are God's children now; what we will be has not been revealed" (1 John 3:2). The Church's tradition has understood this Johannine verse as the eschatological parallel to the creation of human beings in God's image and likeness; human beings will be given a new life; of the exact content of that new life, we are as yet unsure.

No one has said better than St. Irenaeus that for human beings to truly live is to see God:

Just as those who see the light are in the light and share in its splendor, so those who see God are in God and share in his splendor. The splendor of God is lifegiving. So those who see God will share in Life. Such is why the imperceptible, incomprehensible, and invisible God let himself be seen, understood and perceived by human beings: in order to give life to those who perceive and see him. For, if his grandeur is inscrutable, his goodness is also inexpressible, and it is thanks to this that he lets himself be seen and that he gives life to those who see him. For it is impossible to live without life, and there is no other life except through participation in God, and this participation in God consists in seeing him and rejoicing in his goodness. Thus human beings see God in order to live, becoming immortal by this vision and reaching up to God. . . . The glory of God is a living human being and the life of a human being is the vision of God. If the revelation of God through creatures already gives life to all that lives, how much more will the manifestation of the Father through the Word give life to those who see God.[1]

The Church's tradition calls this vision "beatific" because it is the vision of God's glory and because it brings with it the fullness of happiness. This happiness does not consist only in the realization of all human aspirations, but goes beyond them: "What no eye has seen, nor ear heard, nor the human heart conceived, what God has prepared for those who love him" (1 Cor 2:9); this is what God's wisdom has revealed to us and what is promised to us in glory. For God is "able to accomplish abundantly far more than all we can ask or imagine" (Eph 3:20).

Inevitable Images

We cannot speak of what is beyond all human experience except through a network of complementary images. This use of images is inevitable, but the images must be understood for what they are. For example, the image of seeing in relation to God does not imply a simple spectacle, an interminable "incessant 'One God Show' which takes place in an eternal boredom."[2] It is rather a seeing which is the fullness of life. Think of the

---

1. Irenaeus of Lyons, *Against the Heresies*, trans. D. J. Unger (New York: Paulist, 1992) 6:33.

2. P. Guilbert, *Il ressucita le troisième jour* (Paris: Centurion, 1975) 251.

great sights we may have experienced, transitory though they may be: communion with an entrancing landscape, saturated in beauty, which produces joy for the heart as well as for the eye; the artistic wonder produced by the color and form of a picture; the fragile beauty of a beloved person. We speak in these cases of "being ravished"; it is as though we are torn from ourselves by a spark of transcendence which points us to the absolute.

We may also think of the experience of our senses of hearing, touching, smelling, and tasting. Eternal life is thus presented as a festive meal; this image no doubt evokes the pleasure of taste but is also inseparable from that of conviviality, of human exchange which occurs through the sharing of food. The meal is evoked in the gospel parables as the wedding feast of the Son with humanity. The metaphor of wedding sends us back to the greatest experiences of love, which too is an image of the life of love which will be ours through our participation in the Trinitarian relationship.

The book of Revelation presents heaven in the image of an eternal liturgy celebrated around the throne of God and of the slain and glorious Lamb. We must not introduce into the image the perspective of a wearying celebration which never ends, but rather the intensity of celebration, of an exceptional instant which never passes.

Scripture also uses the images of the Holy City, of the heavenly Jerusalem, described in the book of Revelation (21:3-4) in which

> He will dwell with them as their God
> they will be his peoples,
> and God himself will be with them;
> he will wipe every tear from their eyes.
> Death will be no more;
> mourning and crying and pain will be no more,
> for the first things have passed away.

Another image is that of the promised land where milk and honey flow without end.

Evidently, we should not make heaven the place of an egoistic and debased rejoicing from the use of such images. The joy of heaven will no doubt have something absolutely different from earthly pleasure about it. Otherwise it could not fulfill us, nor be to our taste. It will be the presence of a perfectly pure love, open to others, which invites us to continual self transcendence, to an ever greater openness and communion.

A Vision of St. Teresa

They told me of the death of a religious who had been provincial of our province and who, at the time of his death governed another province. I had had dealings with him and was indebted to him for some good deeds. He was a person of great virtue. Yet as soon as I learned of his death a great feeling of anxiety overtook me: I feared for his salvation. For twenty years he had been superior, something I fear because I think that there is a lot of danger in being responsible for others' souls. In great affliction I betook myself to an oratory. I offered up for him all the good I had done in my life, even though it was very little, and I asked the Lord to supply from his own merits what was necessary for that soul to be freed from purgatory. While beseeching the Lord for this as best I could, it seemed to me that I saw this soul on my right, coming out of the depths of the earth and rising up to heaven, filled with the greatest happiness. This religious was very old at the moment of his death but I saw him with the features of a man of about thirty or even less, and his countenance was resplendent. The vision passed very quickly, but I was so consoled that his death could never cause me any more sorrow, although many others felt great sorrow at his death as he was much esteemed. The consolation my soul experienced was so great that I was completely at peace about him and could not doubt the reality of the vision. That is to say, I was not the victim of an illusion.

No more than fifteen days had passed since his death. However, I didn't neglect to get others to pray for him and to pray for him myself, except that I couldn't do it with the same eagerness I would have had if I had not seen this vision. When the Lord shows people to me in this way and afterwards when I desire to pray for them, it seems like giving alms to the rich. As this religious died in a place a great distance from here, I only learned later what a holy death the Lord granted him. His death was very edifying; all those who were present were much impressed with the lucidity of spirit, the tears and humility in which he died.

(St. Teresa Of Avila, *Autobiography*)

Heaven, a Community of Persons

If heaven is communion of human beings with God, it is evidently also communion of human beings among themselves. Humanity is made up of a "multitude of sisters and brothers." Heaven is made by the mystical body of Christ, the body of humanity integrated into the personal humanity of Christ. Heaven is thus the perfect realization of the Church which thus becomes one with the kingdom of God that it announced and worked to develop on earth.

From this point, in "heaven," the walls of hatred are overthrown: humanity lives in complete reconciliation and love. All the relationships begun on earth continue again and develop in fullness in heaven where an infinite number of new relationships begin. This communion without confusion finds its life in the very unity of the Father, Son, and Spirit and exists to their praise and glory. This is why the Church honors the saints, those witnesses to the gospel who, by their example and their teaching, help us to journey toward the kingdom. Glorified in the presence of the Father, they do not cease to associate their intercession with that of Christ. In such a concert, the Virgin Mary is the first to pray for us.

This is only possible because the distinction between human persons is perfectly maintained, as is the unique, concrete identity of each. The disproportion between God and human beings may raise a perplexing question for us. In the universe of the kingdom of God, shall we not be lost like a drop of water in the sea? What will become of our personality? Will not this gift of God diminish us to the point of nonexistence? Do not the Eastern mystics present salvation as a form of self-loss in the great All?

This is not so, according to the Christian vision. The divinization of human beings, already secretly lived through grace and which will be fully manifested in the glory of God, is never in conflict with their humanization. The two coincide since we cannot be fully ourselves except by living in communion with God. The nearness of God to human beings does not result in our loss but in our animation; we become more free and more ourselves.

All that goes into making our identity as men and women, an identity created by our earthly history, will be maintained, while at the same time being transfigured. The personal being which has been fashioned, the richness of our experiences, the knowledge and insights gained during our life, all of which is the fruit of grace and our personal freedom, we will keep possession. Heaven shall be thus the "refinding" of the human relationships established on earth. God will take our incomplete beings and give them new dimensions beyond what we can dream.

A New Heaven and a New Earth

We know neither the moment of the consummation of the earth and of human beings nor the way the universe will be transformed. The form of this world, distorted by sin, is passing away and we are taught that God is preparing a new dwelling and a new earth in which righteousness dwells, whose happiness will fill and surpass all the desires of peace arising in the hearts of human beings. Then, with death conquered, the sons of God will be raised in Christ and what was sown in weakness and dishonor will put on the imperishable: charity and its works will remain, and all of creation, which God made for human beings, will be set free from its bondage to decay.

We have been warned, of course, that it profits human beings nothing if they gain the whole world and lose or forfeit themselves. Far from diminishing our concern to develop this earth, the expectancy of a new earth should spur us on, for it is here that the body of a new human family grows, foreshadowing in some way the age which is to come. That is why, although we must be careful to distinguish earthly progress clearly from the increase of the kingdom of Christ, such progress is of vital concern to the kingdom of God, insofar as it can contribute to the better ordering of human society.

When we have spread on earth the fruits of our nature and our ingenuity—human dignity, human communion and freedom—according to the Lord's command and in his Spirit, we will find them once again, cleansed this time from the stain of sin, illuminated and transfigured, when Christ presents to his Father an eternal and universal kingdom "of truth and life, a kingdom of holiness and grace, a kingdom of justice, love and peace." Here on earth the kingdom is mysteriously present; when the Lord comes it will enter into its perfection.

(Pastoral Constitution on the Church in the Modern World)

But what of tiny children or the mentally handicapped whose intelligence could not function on earth? Will they too experience a veritable expansion of personality or will they be the "poor relations" of heaven? We know that the greatly handicapped are capable of living rich lives and are not deprived of relationships. Their passage into God will be first of all a liberation of their handicap, as well as a healing of all their faculties of understanding and loving. The following marvellous reflection is attributed to General de Gaulle and was made to his wife after the burial of their daughter, Anne, who was a Down's syndrome child upon whom they bestowed much affection: "Now she is like the others." In heaven, a handicapped child will be "like the others," and the development of their freedom which could not be manifested on earth will be richly manifested in heaven.

From Beginning to Beginning

The life of human beings in God will not be a static and monotone reality; it will be a perpetual growth in knowledge and love. Gregory of Nyssa, a fourth-century father of the Church, allows us to evoke it through this well-known text:

> Thus the one who mounts never stops going from beginning to beginning, by beginnings which never end. The one who ascends never ceases to desire that which they already know, but successively rising by another desire, again greater, to another still greater desire, the soul pursues its route towards the infinite through ever greater ascensions.[3]

Heaven Anticipated

At present the new world is in gestation—it grows without ceasing around us until the day of the full revelation and transfiguration of everything in God. Until the end of time, heaven is a house with open doors.

But, one may think, does not this idyllic representation of the happiness promised us in the future kingdom risk making us forget that the kingdom of heaven is already present here on earth—

3. Gregory of Nyssa, *Canticle of Canticles,* trans. C. McCanbley (Brookline, Mass.: Hellenistic College Press, 1987).

indeed has been present since the coming of Christ—and that it demands numerous tasks. Should we not say to ourselves what was said by the angels of the Ascension, "Men of Galilee, why do you stand looking up toward heaven?" (Acts 1:11). Without doubt, such a temptation has afflicted Christians in former times more than Christians today. In the measure that it is true, we must never forget that heaven eternalizes all the acts of love and service that human beings accomplish on earth. According to God's plan, heaven will be constituted partly by what we have done. This is why such a perspective must be translated into an awareness of an urgency to act in faith, hope, and love, so that human beings may become more human and may open themselves to God. In this sense the constitution of the earthly city also builds upon the heavenly city. However, we must not allow the weight of eternity, which is attached to each of our actions, to overwhelm us by its grandeur. Rather, it must sow deep in us a call to work for the salvation of the world.

In the measure that our life grows in faith, we must not be inattentive to the signs, though they may be fragile and tentative, of the anticipation of heaven on earth. Such signs are at work wherever human beings repent, renounce their sin, and discover love, and wherever the struggle for justice, freedom, and respect for the rights of each exists. It is not for nothing that the images of heaven are taken from the earth. These signs are only the visible face of that hidden gestation of the kingdom of heaven among us.

10

Purgatory: A Healing

The term *purgatory,* unfortunately, has developed bad connotations as the metaphors used to describe it are usually naive and simplistic, if not cruel and perverse. This is unfortunate because, in fact, purgatory designates a very positive doctrine and phenomenon. This gap between perception and reality is great enough that finding a new name for it has been frequently discussed. With these complications in mind, we shall with discretion examine the history and doctrine of purgatory in a hopefully more fruitful way.

False and Even Dangerous Representations

The current image of purgatory that dwells in our minds and sometimes in our unconscious is of a place of *suffering* in which human beings—who are already God's friends, yet still weighed down with the weight of the consequences of their sins—*expiate* their sins during a designated amount of *time,* so as to satisfy divine justice through this compensation. The conventional wisdom is that purgatory is a place where one goes to "expiate" one's debt, in light of what one has done.

In this place of suffering and torment the dungeon keeper would certainly be God. Purgatory is understood analagously in relation to the images of hell; in both cases one burns, but the great difference is that the first does not last forever, but is only for a certain time.

This conception rests on an idea of God's justice, which is a projection into the beyond of the inadequate justice of human beings. The condemned are sent to prison where they are purged of their debts before being readmitted into society. This punishment is both vindictive, that is, repressive (we know of what certain political regimes have been capable in regard to prisoners) and corrective, for it aims to lead the delinquent back to the right road. And, as all in the beyond must be pushed to the extreme, this time of "detention" in purgatory is replete with an array of methods of pain.

This type of image is perverse because, taking up the image of a concentration camp, it makes God the supreme and consummate S.S. officer. The irony in this system of thought is that human beings project onto God their own conception of justice, which is marked by sin. We know Voltaire's ironic word: "They say that God made human beings in his own image; human beings have done the same to him." Such is the case in this conception of purgatory, itself linked in modern times to a false idea of the sacrifice on the cross. Here God is seen as vindictive and in search of retribution. This image of God is, of course, unfortunate as it contradicts so much of what Scripture tells us about God's justice—that it is based upon kindness, justice, and is life-affirming. Nevertheless, this God of retribution was emphasized at times in Church history and, unfortunately, has had a lasting effect.

There is also a certain naivety in representing purgatory as a place and a time analogous to those of our universe. For God's universe is that of mutual presence, where partitions no longer have reason to exist. Eternity is not a succession of instants but a simultaneous presence to all in a unique instant which is forever. When human beings leave this earthly life, they pass immediately into this universe which does not share our chronological organization. By all means possible, we must go beyond this sort of representation so as to understand purgatory as an aspect or a dimension of the passage of human beings into God.

The Birth and Development of Purgatory

It is interesting to note that we do not find a doctrine of purgatory—at least one in which it is understood to be an interim place of purgation—until the twelfth century. Until then the word was used only as an adjective. Since the time of Augustine, one spoke of a "purifying fire."[1] This historical fact explains the divergence between the Catholic and Orthodox Churches on this matter. In the same way, the Churches which issued from the Reformation, by reason of their biblical principle and their reaction against the abuses of indulgences, do not believe in the existence of purgatory.

How can we explain this development? Two major factors must be highlighted: the value of prayer for the dead, and the conviction of the need for the majority of the deceased to undergo purification so that they may eventually appear before God. These two themes are linked and qualify one another.

Prayer for the Dead

The well-known adage, *lex orandi, lex credendi,* which posits that the rule of prayer is the rule of faith, plays a major role here. Already in the Judaism of the first century B.C., one prayed for the dead. So it was that Judas Maccabeus prayed and even offered sacrifice for the soldier who died in battle and who was suspected of apostasy:

> So they all blessed the ways of the Lord, the righteous judge, who reveals the things that are hidden; and they turned to supplication, praying that the sin that had been committed might be wholly blotted out. The noble Judas exhorted the people to keep themselves free from sin, for they had seen with their own eyes what had happened as the result of the sin of those who had fallen. He also took up a collection, man by man, to the amount of two thousand drachmas of silver, and sent it to Jerusalem to provide for a sin offering. In doing this he acted very well and honorably, taking account of the resurrection. For if he were not expecting that those who had fallen would rise again, it would have been superfluous and foolish to pray for the dead. But he was looking to the splendid reward that is laid up for those who fall asleep in godliness, it was a holy and pious thought. Therefore he made atonement for the dead, so that they might be delivered from their sin (2 Macc 12:41-45).

1. Cf. J. Le Goff, *The Birth of Purgatory,* trans. Arthur Goldhammer (Chicago: University of Chicago Press, 1984).

The author of this text praises three qualities in Judas Maccabeus' gesture: his hope in the resurrection; his hope in God's forgiveness of those who died at the end of an uncertain life; and for the ability of the living to intercede on behalf of the second.

Such practices evolved and were practiced naturally among the early Christians. Thus in the account of the passion of St. Perpetua, in the third century, an account in which the saint sees in a dream her young brother, Dinocratus, recently deceased from cancer at the age of seven. Suffering from thirst and unable to quench his thirst, Perpetua prays for him daily; eventually she is consoled in a dream by the vision of her young brother drinking water and playing joyfully with it as young children do.[2] This image teaches us the effectiveness of prayer for those in need of it.

Similarly, St. Cyprian is preoccupied with the salvation of those who have fallen into apostasy without the opportunity to obtain the reconciliation of the Church, and for those who obtained it only at the last moment. His conviction is that these people are able to be purified after death, and so must be the object of the Church's prayer.[3] The liturgy, for its part, from very early times, included a prayer for the dead through intercession on behalf of the communion of saints.

Cyril of Jerusalem expresses the value of the commemoration of the dead in the Eucharistic liturgy in a double sense:

> Then we also make mention of those who have fallen asleep, first for the patriarchs, prophets, apostles, and martyrs, that God may receive our supplications on account of their prayers and intercessions. Then we pray for the holy fathers and bishops who have fallen asleep, and in general for all those who have fallen asleep before us, believing that this will be for the great profit of their souls, for whom supplication is offered, while the holy and unsurpassing victim is present.[4]

2. *Passion of Saint Perpetua,* trans. J. Armitage Robinson (Liechtenstein: Kraus, 1967).

3. Cyprian, Bishop of Carthage, *The Letters of St. Cyprian,* trans. G. W. Clarke (New York: Newman, 1986) 55:20.

4. Cyril of Jerusalem, "Mystagogical Catecheses," *Fathers of the Church* 64 (Washington: The Catholic University of America Press, 1970).

Thus, according to this testimony, just as the elect intercede fruitfully for human beings who are on earth, so they can intercede usefully for those who have preceded them in death.

St. Augustine also affirms the efficacy of prayer for the dead. He himself prays ardently for his mother St. Monica.[5] He also has the idea of "purifying punishment" for those who have died without being "entirely good," for the struggles of those on earth can help the dead.

What Can Be the Efficacy of Prayer for the Dead?

This prayer for the dead raises difficulties. How can we attribute an efficacy to it if we judge that it cannot change God's judgment about individuals; and how is it effective if it is impossible for us to act in the place of another's freedom? We know how, in the sixteenth century, the abusive and odious practice of indulgences transmitted the idea that an offering could immediately deliver a soul from purgatory. As one preacher used to say, "As soon as the coin is in the collecting box, the soul escapes from purgatory."

In reality, these difficulties touch the question of the fruitfulness of any prayer for others. We cannot pretend to change God's attitude in regard to the person for whom we pray, since his benevolence is always present to them; we do not have power over their interior liberty. But here the difficulty is increased since the relationship between the here and now and the beyond of eternity is introduced.

The answer to these questions is to be found in the reality of the communion of saints and in the fecundity of love. Belief in the communion of saints affirms a spiritual solidarity between all those who belong to the one body of Christ and in which the circulation of life is entirely directed by the head. We can understand something of this from the solidarity of human freedoms which we may experience here on earth. Any evil committed in our world affects the wider society, whether by its example or by its consequences. It makes the practice of good more difficult for us. On the other hand, the person who aims high also raises others and the world. The development of the freedom of each

5. Augustine, *Confessions,* IX. 13. 34–37.

is thus conditioned by the use of freedom by all. The child has need of the love of its parents if it is to love and to use its freedom well; we all have need of the love of others to live and to progress. Salvation respects this fundamental solidarity.

The solidarity between the members of the body of Christ crosses the threshold of death. On the one hand, all the elect who belong to the glorified body of Christ unite themselves in their praise and thanksgiving to him "since he always lives to make intercession for them" (Heb 7:25). This great movement of love in saved humanity supports our freedom and helps it to act in love. This is why we are able to confide ourselves to the intercession of the Virgin and the saints, whose intercession has value only when joined to Christ's intercession. This intercession of Christ and the saints evidently helps all those who have to live through a process of purification before seeing God. But the pilgrim Church is not at the door of this great moment of communication in love; this is why its members must pray for one another in praise and thanksgiving. This prayer is for those who share our earthly life, and especially for those who are undergoing their final combat so that this may successfully find its fulfillment in a death in Christ and their whole person and destiny be taken up to Christ. It is the unbreakable unity constituted by their earthly life and their passage into God which is the object of our prayer, beyond all temporal needs. When we celebrate the Eucharist for the dead, we give thanks to the Father through Jesus Christ for the wonders he has worked in them. We then unite our intercession for them to that of Christ, which is an act of communion with them in the one love of Christ.

A Sanctifying Purification

A passage from 1 Corinthians 3:11-15 has contributed much to the development of the doctrine of purgatory, even though its interpretation in the traditional sense is disputed today:

> For no one can lay any foundation other than the one that has been laid; that foundation is Jesus Christ. Now if anyone builds on the foundation with gold, silver, precious stones, wood, hay straw—the work of each builder will become visible, for the Day will disclose it, because it will be revealed with fire, and the fire

will test what sort of work each has done. If what has been built on the foundation survives, the builder will receive a reward. If the work is burned up, the builder will suffer loss; the builder will be saved, but only as through fire.

We must not seek an illustration of naive images of purgatory in this text, "But, to the contrary, does not 'purgatory' find its true Christian definition when we give it a Christological sense and when we explain that the Lord himself is the fire which judges human beings in the very act of transforming them and conforming them to his glorified body?" (Rom 8:29; Phil 3:21).[6]

Whatever this text may mean, Scripture insists that we must have pure hearts when we approach God: "Blessed are the pure in heart, for they will see God!" (Matt 5:8). Our reconciliation with God, achieved through the death of his Son, has as its goal to "present you holy and blameless and irreproachable before him" (Col 1:22). Christ gave himself up for the Church, "in order to make her holy by cleansing her with the washing of water by the word, so as to present the Church to himself in splendor, without a spot or wrinkle or anything of the kind—yes, so that she may be holy and without blemish" (Eph 5:25-27).

It was with this sole term of *purification* that Vatican II discreetly evoked the doctrine of purgatory (*Lumen Gentium* 49). In the light of its history, how should we understand this doctrine today?

"Operation Truth" (H. Bourgeois[7])

Purgatory is a process of purification, an operation which creates truth in us and which makes us stand in the truth so that we may come to the blessed vision of God and thus to the fullness of life.

This "process," which we tend to think of as a "time," takes place, by definition, outside of time, since it belongs to the "beyond." It must rather be considered as a qualitative aspect of our passage into God and of the personal judgment of each person. The "moment" of purgatory is that of our encounter with God.

6. J. Ratzinger, *La mort et l'au-delà* (Paris, Fayard, 1979) 248.
7. H. Bourgeois, *L'espérance maintenant et toujours* (Paris: Desclée, 1985) 262-63.

The Fire of Love Is Always the Same

The doctrine of purgatory is founded on the belief that to be united to God in a communion of life we must be total love as he is all love. Not an atom, not a grain of egoism can enter into God. Only love can be assimilated to love. Who thus would dare to think that at the hour of their death they were established in perfect love and that there was not the slightest atom of egoism in them? This is impossible; the Virgin Mary is the only exception.

Let us express this clearly in a play on words. In order that love be consummated in beatitude, egoism must be consumed in the repentance of purification.

Such purification teaches that the deepest depths of the being cannot but be painful.

To be torn away from oneself is the pinnacle of suffering. The suffering we experience at present is the beginning of this purifying work. And if suffering did not have this value of purification, it would be simply a non-sense, a scandal. There is, therefore, a purgatory which begins here on earth.

It is not surprising that the tradition compares the burning of purification to a fire.

Purgatory also signifies purifying. At root, it is the same fire which damns in hell, which purifies in purgatory, and which beatifies in heaven. God does not change; the fire of love is always the same. It is we who are different in the presence of infinite and immutable love: if we are in a condition of being, which is the total opposite of love, God's fire will torture us; if we are capable of purification, this fire will purify us; and if we are united to God, this fire will beatify us.

(Francois Varillon, *Joie de croire, joie de vivre,* conferences collected by Bernard Housset, Le Centurion, 1981, 203)

But why is this purification? Because even if the fundamental orientation of our life has responded positively to God's grace, we remain entangled in sin—the pride, violence, and lies with which we continue to struggle. There are still resistances in us, deep zones of our being which are not yet fully converted. Our personality is not yet completely integrated into the dynamic of love.

We need to look at our lives with courage if we are to discover that which we hide from others. Very often we are incapable of carrying the weight of truth by which others would judge us. But God's world is a world of light and transparency and we cannot enter it without becoming transparent and light-filled ourselves.

The necessity of purgatory originates, therefore, in us and not in an arbitrary will of God.

Why Suffering?

The suffering of purgatory is that of a love still bound. The still impure gold of our love must be put in the fire to be purified of all its impurities. And God is that "devouring fire" (Deut 4:24) whose love consumes all that is opposed to it. We have, for example, to purify our sensibility and our imagination: "Death and resurrection sound like the awakening of our deep sensitivity which is more or less asleep while we are on earth. . . . We receive straight into our hearts all the blows that we have dealt others."[8] We call a time of intense conversion a moment of fire. This fire is both that of contrition and of love—suffering for not having loved enough is transformed into love.

We also have to be purified of the false ideas that we create of God and of others, and be liberated from the unhealthy sufferings to which we cling: "Each may suffer, even terribly, from a punishment they will never undergo, but which tortures them interiorly and about which they agonize. This is a gross misunderstanding, so much the more when one amplifies in one's imagination the force of the brutal blow that one will never receive."[9]

The suffering of purgatory is correlative to the dispossession of self that needs to happen so that we can see things as God sees them. Paradoxically, this suffering is also a joy, a "contentment," says St. Catherine of Genoa; it is the joy of entry into the light and into life.

8. D. Foucher, *Répose aux questions: Dieu, Satan, l'au-delà, la résurrection, le purgatoire, la femme?* (1984) 77.

9. Ibid., 79.

Purgatory, Gift of God

From God's side, purgation is not punishment; it is the gift of transformation. At the same time, it is one of the demands of God's love. As the father met the prodigal son, so God meets us with open arms and then clothes us with the best robe. He cannot allow his children to enter the family home dirty and dressed in rags. To enter the banquet of the king, one must be clothed in the wedding garment.

Purgatory is thus the expression of God's great patience which holds out the possibility of the achievement of our full conversion to love, right up until we reach beyond earthly life. Let us not try to find any opposition between justice and mercy in God. His justice is merciful and his mercy is just.

In this purifying encounter with God, the role of Christ, the incarnate and risen Son, is central. The one who saved us by his paschal mystery, purifies us and thus integrates us definitively into his glorified body. God regards us only through the face of his Son, as St. Thérese of the Child Jesus understood.

11

Hell? A Tragic Possibility

A reflection on the future of our life in God cannot dismiss the question of hell even if it is a dramatic, painful theme, full of terrible images which seem to present God as a policeman, an avenger who takes a sadistic pleasure in punishing. One thing is certain: without forgetting the teachings of the Church, but without seeking to know everything, we have to let our ideas on the subject be transformed.

Our point of departure is the most central and unshakeable certitude of our faith: God is love. We cannot think of the hypothesis of hell outside of this perspective. Nothing in the New Testament texts contradicts this affirmation of God's absolute and universal love. This is to say that God *does not want* hell, this tragic and definitive rejection of love.

But human beings may want not to love; it is this possibility that gives birth to the idea of hell. If Scripture evokes a hell with images of suffering, it is not to satisfy curiosity, not to describe in detail the condition of future reprobates, still less to say how many they will be. Scripture intends simply to put us on our guard. Human existence, then, is one in which we are given the choice of loving or refusing to love. Hell is a real possibility for each of us, if our freedom rejects God in a definitive manner. This warning does not tell us there is anyone in hell. It does not take away from us the hope that all will be saved, according to God's universal plan (cf. 1 Tim 2:4).

Hell in the Preaching of Jesus

The long arc of revelation which stretches from the depths of the underworld *(sheol* or *hades)* to hell has already been described.[1] The underworld of the Old Testament represented the general lot of human beings until the moment when hope in salvation and resurrection was born. With the proclamation of the definitive victory over death gained by Jesus, hell is only a possibility for those who formally refuse salvation.

That is why Jesus' preaching in the Gospels puts us in a situation of having to choose between good and evil, between love of God and neighbor and egoistic and proud refusal which turns human beings in on themselves. It puts us on guard by telling us that two issues are possible. In this, Jesus does not hesitate to use the most violent Jewish scriptural images and representations: "the furnace of fire," "weeping and gnashing of teeth" (Matt 13:42); "hell, where the worm never dies, and the fire is never quenched" (Mark 9:47-48). It is the Lord who says to the foolish virgins "I do not know you" (Matt 25:12) and who demands that the lazy and egoistic servant should be thrown out into "the outer darkness" (Matt 25:30); and Jesus himself will be the Son of Man who has the authority to say, "Depart from me into the eternal fire . . ." (Matt 25:41). The one "who does not believe will be condemned" (Mark 16:16). In John's Gospel, too, Jesus castigates the world which will not believe.

However, these images of hell are often tied to parabolic texts. We must not "read them as if they were an anticipated report of what would happen one day, but as the revelation of the true present situation in which questioned human beings find themselves. It is the situation of a subject placed before a decision of irreversible consequences; of those who may be definitively lost if they refuse the offer of salvation which God makes to them."[2]

If it is such, how should we understand the gospel word, "For many are called but few are chosen" (Matt 22:14)? Jesus' reflection must be seen in the context of the Old Testament theme of a "small remnant" which describes the stages of salvation in a generalized way. It does not pretend to give "statistical proportions"[3] of the elect and of the damned. Even its logic in-

1. Cf. ch. 2, "The birth and development of faith in the resurrection," pp. 15-22.

2. K. Rahner, *Sacramentum mundi* (New York: Herder, 1968-70) 2:736.

3. Cf. the study of D. Foucher on the small number of the elect in *Pourquoi l'enfer, si Dieu est amour?* (Montligeon, 1986) 161-215.

vites us to radicalize it: the "many" signifies *all* (just as Jesus sheds his blood for "the many" (Mark 10:45; 14:24), and *few* signifies that *no one* is automatically saved, independent of one's response. Once again we are in the presence of a warning, not statistics. Over time this verse has fueled speculation about the "small number of the elect"; such discourses, which are replete in the Augustinian notion of the "mass of the damned," continue through the medieval conception of hell and its inhabitance, and have been experienced in our century through the severe preaching of modern times. These "theologies of terror" have sometimes developed into the excesses of the doctrine of predestination, a doctrine formally condemned by the Church, as if God predestined to evil and to damnation those who would refuse salvation. This tradition, especially as it has come down to us in its Jansonistic form, is, in many ways, an obstacle to faith.

Hell: A Real Risk for Every Created Liberty

The first meaning of this gospel warning is to remind us that the God who is love cannot, by definition, impose on our freedom; instead, he offers himself in order to be recognized and welcomed. It is possible that he will not be welcomed by a fully free and responsible choice that, in fact, he may be totally and definitively rejected. This is the foundation on which the possibility of hell is based.

Edith Stein, a Carmelite nun who died in a World War II concentration camp and was recently beatified, wrote, "It belongs to the soul to decide for itself. The great mystery which the freedom of the person constitutes is that God himself waits before this liberty. He only wishes to rule created spirits, those who choose to love God out of freedom."[4] The divine liberty cannot be limited except by the liberty of human beings.

To totally refuse God's love is to definitively reject the Holy Spirit. Jesus says, "Therefore I tell you, people will be forgiven for every sin and blasphemy, but blasphemy against the Spirit will not be forgiven . . . either in this age or in the age to come" (Matt 12:31-32). For the sin against the Holy Spirit is both the sin against

4. Edith Stein, *The Science of the Cross* (Chicago: Regnery, 1960).

the light, against life (for it is the Spirit who gives life), and against love.

It seems that here we come up against an unjust and untenable disproportion: how can a finite liberty, conditioned as it is, and always exercising itself in particular choices, choose and seal an eternal destiny? The same question may be asked of freedom itself: "Freedom is not really the possibility of always being able to reverse decisions, but the power of the definitive, the power of the subject who . . . must be brought to their definitive and irrevocable state; . . . freedom is the power of what is eternal. . . . Freedom is the act of the eternal."[5] If we question our experience, do we not discover this at the heart of our commitments to love and freedom? If it is not thus, it must be said that we are not free. The possibility of hell is inversely proportional to our desire to construct the definitive by a freely chosen love.

Hell Is a Creation of Human Beings

From this perspective hell is no longer God's punishment, but the creation of human beings. God does not make hell; hell is made manifest when love is refused.

Our experience here on earth gives us an idea of what the reality of hell could be. Hell is already on earth when hatred, egoism, violence, injustice, and the overriding desire for money are uppermost. This is an existence without love; it is aggressive confrontation, the law of survival of the fittest, and contempt of the other. It is incarceration in a solitude contrary to the social nature of human beings. Sartre's formula in *Huis-Clos* is well known: "Hell is other people." The country priest in Bernanos's novel says for his part, "Hell, Madame, is not to love anymore."

Another form of hell is despair, the moment when a blocked horizon no longer opens onto a future, when life appears denuded of all value and meaning, and is no longer worth living. "To despair is to descend into hell," said Isidore of Seville.[6]

In our century, cold and calculated hate has organized hell in Nazi concentration camps and in the gulags of too many countries, wherein the detainees of these places become the damned

---

5. K. Rahner, *Traité fondamental de la foi* (Paris: Centurion, 1983) 115.
6. Cf. J. Piper, *Über die Hoffnung* (Leipzig: Hegner, 1935) 49.

of the earth. But are not those who invent these worlds of torture the more truly damned?

No doubt, none of these hells is fixed and definite: hope can exist among those imprisoned in a concentration camp, or among the downtrodden of an urban slum. And, of course, there is always the possibility that the heart of a torturer will be converted and, thus, victims will be saved. Yet these different hells show us of what human beings are capable.

Hell, the image of which comes from the Christian narrative, must not be understood as a refinement of tortures sadistically invented by God, but as the result of an intentional rejection of love. The so-called "pain of the damned" is, in fact, the suffering endured by those who have no hope of seeing and loving God. Hell is to be deprived of that which humans need most—the love and desire of God—for, what we lack in love of God, we lack in love of neighbor as well. That is, one of life's supreme ironies is that those who hate God, hate themselves for hating God, for, in actuality, they desire God. As a result, they are consumed by a perpetual, internal battle. The other suffering such people endure is a symptom of this reality.

Must Hell Be Eternal?

The greatest difficulty posed by hell is the question of its eternity. Can the human family be totally happy if certain members are excluded from the possibility of salvation? Would not the presence of hell, of even one condemned person, be a scandal to God himself? How is an eternal hell compatible with the logic of a God of absolute love, a God who desires that all be saved? How can brothers and sisters of Christ, created by the Father, and for whom the Son died on a cross, be condemned for eternity?

There was a variety of Church fathers, including Origen, Clement of Alexandria, and Gregory of Nyssa, who were concerned with this issue, and so theologized that there will be a time of "reestablishment," or restitution of everything at the end of time.[7] They thought that the end of the universe was accountable to the

---

7. The technical term is *apocatastase,* a Greek word which means "reestablishment," or "recovery," which is found in Acts 3:21.

beginning of time—God's creation of the world—and that all creation, then, would be put in its original order.

The Risk of Freedom

Neither hell, nor purgatory, nor original sin are intelligible outside the human vocation to divinization.

The respect God has for our liberty, which is essential to love, includes the possibility of hell, but a possibility which the reality and solidity of salvation makes us consider in hope. Fidelity is not a certainty of mathematical order.

Risk has the same amplitude as liberty, and all that you can do to diminish the risk diminishes liberty at the same time.

If hell is a reality, the reality of damnation, it is not the reality of a volcano. We ought not to talk of "hell" because the word evokes a place in people's minds. Hell is a state of damnation, which is a real possibility, but I cannot affirm that it is a reality. The great risk finally, is that if damnation is real and not only a possibility, . . . it is first of all a grief for God, and we think very little of this.

One could say many things but I prefer to be prudent in this area. I admit that it is scarcely thinkable at the limit, but the risk is real. Finally, I cannot think that God can manipulate us in the end. God's love must be straightforwardly pure, or God would say implicitly: "My poor friend, . . . finally I arranged to save you in spite of all." I fear that there would be a degradation in God's mercy and love. In other words, I ask myself if the sublimity of the Christian vocation does not also imply the possibility of tragedy. If you suppress the tragic, does the sublime remain sublime? It is for this reason that outside of our vocation to share in the divine life hell is inconceivable.

(Francois Varillon [Exchanges with Charles Ehlinger], *Beauté du monde et souffrance des hommes* [Paris: *Le Centurion,* 1980] 130–31)

In fact, the Church has always rejected such a thesis. For in its eyes the "success at any price" of God's work, which would not respect human liberty, would annihilate both God's work and human liberty. Humanity would be no more than a great robot, led toward an inevitable beatitude—and thus without value. God's love would lose itself in the almighty power of an apparently grandiose realization, but deprived of all soul and meaning. As paradoxical as it might appear, an eternity of hell is a corollary of God's love of human liberty.

The Right and the Duty to Hope on Behalf of All

> Love bears all things, believes all things, endures all things
> (1 Cor 13:7).

Hell is thus a dramatic possibility open to our freedom. Can we conclude that there are people in hell and may we go so far as to say if they are numerous or not? Certainly not. The silence of Scripture is total on this point, even in the case of Judas, who was guilty of betrayal: "Neither holy Scripture, nor the tradition of the Church, say clearly of any person that they are to be found in hell. But hell appears constantly as a *real possibility,* under the same title as the possibility of being converted and of receiving life."[8]

There is a paradox which is sometimes translated by the quip, "Hell exists, but there is no one there." In a more just manner we may say in all truth that hell is a real possibility, but we may seriously hope that it will not be the destination of any human person.

This hope is founded on God's desire for universal salvation: "We have to hold together," writes Karl Rahner, "the proposition that God fervently desires universal salvation, that all humanity be saved by Christ, that we must *hope for the salvation of all,* and the proposition that eternal perdition is a real possibility."[9]

Scripture tells us again and again that God wills all to be saved (Rom 11:32; Col 1:19-20; Eph 1:10; John 12:32). Let us keep in mind here three particularly clear affirmations: ". . . God our Savior, who desires everyone to be saved and to come to the knowledge of the truth" (1 Tim 2:4); and "For the grace of God has appeared, bringing salvation to all. . . ."; and "The Lord is not slow about his promise, as some think of slowness, but is patient with you, not wanting any to perish, but all to come to repentance" (2 Pet 3:9).

8. *La foi de l'Eglise,* 409.
9. K. Rahner, *Sacramentum mundi* (New York: Herder, 1968–70) 2:736.

The historical and visible part of the history of salvation, which culminates in the mystery of the cross and resurrection of Jesus, should not lead us to doubt God's saving intentions. Between a "possible" hell and an "actual" hell, there is the untiring, freeing love of God at work so that the catastrophe which could happen may never happen. Such a hope is not simply in the abstract; it concerns concretely all those who are dear to us.

If it is thus, we must not fear hell either for ourselves or for others. We may say with Kierkegaard:

> Of my life, I have never been and, without doubt, shall never be further from the point of "fear and trembling" when I am literally certain that every other being will easily accede to beatitude. To say to others: "You are lost for all eternity" is an impossibility for me. For myself, one thing is clear: all the others will be blessed—and this is enough—for myself alone the outcome remains undecided.[10]

In reality, all speculation about hell for others—with the inference that hell does not concern me because I am saved—is a perversion of the biblical teaching and contrary to love of neighbor. Indeed, it turns me into the pharisee of the parable (Luke 18:11): "Whoever envisages the possibility, even of a *single* reprobate outside of themselves," writes H. Urs von Balthasar, "will find it very difficult to love without reserve."[11]

Such a spiritual attitude can liberate us from the fear of damnation of those we love. We can even imitate the "foolish" prayer of Moses and of St. Paul in which, after the sin that led to the adoration of the golden calf, Moses went up the mountain and prayed: "But now, if you will only forgive their sin—but if not, blot me out of the book that you have written" (Exod 32:32),

---

10. Cited by H. Urs von Balthasar, in *Esperer pour tous* (Paris: Desclée de Brouwer, 1987) 77. This book, one of the last written by H. Urs von Balthasar before his death, is a beautiful meditation on the problem of hell. His thesis was unfairly criticized by some theologians, to whom he responded with a second work which was published posthumously, *L'Enfer. Une question* (Paris: Desclée de Brouwer, 1988). These two works are indispensable references for a contemporary theology of hell.

11. H. Urs von Balthasar, *L'Enfer. Une question* (Paris: Desclée de Brouwer, 1988) 60.

and, in light of Israel's sin, as Paul proclaims, "For I could wish that I myself were accursed and cut off from Christ for the sake of my own people, my kindred according to my flesh" (Rom 9:3). "If you will, forgive their sins. If not, in your mercy, blot me out from the book (of life)" (Exod 32:32). And Paul, remembering Israel's sin, proclaims: "Yes, I desire to be." In this Moses announces, and Paul imitates, Christ who, on the cross, assumed in his body an infernal situation for the salvation of his sisters and brothers, whom he forgave in the persons of his torturers. Such prayers, which take on an evangelical tone, show us that hope is not an obstacle to action; rather, it stimulates that charity which puts us at the service of the salvation of all.

The witnesses of this hope in the Christian tradition are numerous:

> How could I support, Lord, writes Catherine of Siena, that a single one of those you have made like me in your image and likeness, should be lost and escape from your hand? No, in no case do I want a single of my brothers or sisters to be lost, not a single one of those who are united to me by an identical birth, both in nature and in grace.[12]

For St. Thérèse of Lisieux, too, the teaching of the Church on the subject of the possibility of eternal reprobation was a source of great anxiety.[13] Edith Stein, who firmly held that God's freedom accepts its status as "limited by human liberty," reflected lucidly on the case of those who had been seized by death without having thought of their eternity:

> We do not ignore the fact that for innumerable people, temporal death comes without their having thought even for a moment of eternity, and without salvation ever having been a problem for them; that, besides this, many others try to receive the grace without receiving a share in it; nevertheless, we do not know if for both groups the decisive hour will not sound in some eternal beyond, and faith can assure us that all will be well. . . . Thus faith in love and the unlimited grace of God justifies hope in a universality of redemption, even though the possibility of resisting grace— and thus of the possibility of an eternal damnation—remains open.

12. Ibid., 62.
13. Cf. ibid., 63.

Seen from this angle, that which formerly resisted the almighty power of God fall in their turn. . . . It is impossible that human liberty should be broken or excluded by divine liberty, or, as it were, duped by it. The gift of grace to the human soul is a free act of divine love. To its diffusion there are no limits.[14]

Such is also the dominant position among leading theologians today.

Having said this, we can add, "Certitude is not in our grasp, but we may establish hope."[15] We must exorcise our curiosity, which is always in search of assurances. There are no assurances for eternity. We must accept both the terms of the paradox when things do not seem to fit together completely. But are we not seeking knowledge where faith is proposed to us? We want security where hope is demanded of us. We fix ourselves to fear and anguish where we are invited to love.

14. Ibid., 65–67.
15. Ibid., 32.

Our Body
"Sister of Christ"
(Tertullian)

"Men of Galilee, why do you stand looking up toward heaven?" (Acts 1:11); thus spoke the heavenly messengers to the apostles who continued to fix their gaze on high after Jesus' ascension. This ultimate apparition concludes, like those which preceded it, with a commission to mission. The apostles return to Jerusalem to wait for the gift of the Spirit and to begin their work of evangelization according to the Lord's command. The scene of the ascension, like all of Christian life, is marked by this tension between the "above" and "beyond" of our lives, and our being here on earth. This long meditation on the resurrection and eternal life in no way desires to encourage an attitude of flight before the tasks of this world, as if Christians could cross the battlelines, rose in hand. Quite the contrary. Its aim is to make us understand better the eternal consequences of our lives, and to comfort us with the conviction of the loving solidarity which unites all human beings, whether they have crossed the threshold of death or not, a solidarity which may be justly called the communion of saints. Nothing in this world is profane since the Son of God visited it and made it his own; by this act of the Son of God, everything has value and gives birth to the eternal. We do not have to choose between the here and now and the beyond, since the two interpenetrate each other. Eternal life is already here; our life in history carries the weight of eternity. The dismissal of the last realities and of the vocation to life of all and of each human person can only result in underestimating the importance of what happens in our world. On the contrary, a clear vision of the end of the journey gives light and strength to the pilgrim who advances little by little.

Even if it is difficult for all those who are in the midst of distress in the experience of a particularly painful separation, the last word is to be found in faith, hope (we have just seen this in regard to hell) and *love*. Let us borrow from Tertullian the following cry of the heart which holds the secret:

> This body which God fashions in his hands in the image of God, which he animates with his breath, in the likeness of his own life force, that he creates to be part of all its work, to be rejoiced in and given commandments, that he clothed in his mysteries and in his teachings; whose purity he loves, whose mortification he approves, whose very suffering he takes upon himself, will he not raise it, after having been so many times God's? Let the idea be banished that God could abandon to an eternal destruction the work of his hands, the object of his care and his intelligence, the envelope of his breath, the queen of his creation, the inheritor of his liberality, the priest of his religion, the soldier who renders testimony to him, the sister of Christ. We know that God is very good; we know from Christ that he alone is very good. It is he who commands love of neighbor, a love like his own; he thus does himself what he enjoins: he loves the body which is his neighbor under so many titles.[16]

16. Tertullian, *Treatise on the Resurrection,* trans. Ernest Evans (London: S.P.C.K., 1960) 2:807.